JOHN KERRY
Senator from Massachusetts

JOHN KERRY
Senator from Massachusetts

Bruce L. Brager

MORGAN
REYNOLDS
Publishing, Inc.

620 South Elm Street, Suite 223
Greensboro, North Carolina 27406
http://www.morganreynolds.com

JOHN KERRY: SENATOR FROM MASSACHUSETTS

Copyright © 2005 by Bruce L. Brager

Library of Congress Cataloging-in-Publication Data

Brager, Bruce L., 1949-
John Kerry : Senator from Massachusetts / Bruce L. Brager.— 1st ed.
p. cm.
Includes bibliographical references and index.
ISBN-10: 1-931798-64-8 (library binding)
ISBN-13: 978-1-931798-64-8 (library binding)
1. Kerry, John, 1943—Juvenile literature. 2. Legislators—United States—Biography—Juvenile literature. 3. United States. Congress. Senate—Biography—Juvenile literature. I. Title.
E840.8.K427B73 2005
973.931'092—dc22

2005002190

Printed in the United States of America
First Edition

20ᵀᴴ CENTURY LEADERS

JIMMY CARTER

RONALD REAGAN

MARCUS GARVEY

GEORGE W. BUSH

THURGOOD MARSHALL

RICHARD NIXON

LYNDON BAINES JOHNSON

DWIGHT D. EISENHOWER

ISHI

MADELEINE ALBRIGHT

LOU HENRY HOOVER

JOHN KERRY

Contents

Senator John Forbes Kerry.

Chapter One

Family and Youth

It was eleven o'clock on the morning of Wednesday, November 3, 2004, and Senator John Kerry of Massachusetts had to make a difficult telephone call. A little over three months before, he had been nominated by the Democratic Party to be their candidate for president of the United States. It had been a long struggle to win the nomination and, after delivering his acceptance speech at the Democratic Convention, held in his hometown of Boston, many of his supporters were optimistic that he would be able to defeat the incumbent president, George Bush. But that had not happened. After a bitter campaign, the most expensive in U.S. history, John Kerry had been defeated.

Now he had to call President Bush and congratulate him on his victory. It was a difficult call to make, not only because John Kerry was a fierce competitor who hated to lose. He also deeply felt that President Bush's domestic and foreign policies were leading the country in a dangerous direction. During the call, President Bush was gracious and congratulated him for running a good campaign. They discussed their regret that the country had become so divided and agreed to work together to find a way to heal the rift that had led to such a bitter campaign. Then Senator Kerry hung up and turned his attention to thanking his family, friends, and supporters for their hard work. The 2004 presidential campaign was over.

But John Kerry remained a senator from Massachusetts. He had served in the Senate since 1985, which made him one of the leaders of his party and that legislative body. Even if he never became president, John Kerry knew there were many ways to serve his country. It was a lesson he had learned as a child.

One side of Kerry's family traced its roots back to the beginning of the Massachusetts Bay Colony in 1629. His mother's distant ancestor was John Winthrop, the first governor of the colony and the man who first coined the phrase "city upon a hill," which came to represent to many the ultimate symbol of America's promise. Another ancestor on the Forbes side—his mother's—remained loyal to the British during the American Revolution, but the family soon made up for this mistake. In the early 1800s, they helped establish the prosperous trade between the port of Boston and China and remained involved in the business for over a century. It took World War II and the rise to power of the Communists in China to end trade between the two countries.

John Winthrop (1587-1649), the first governor of the Massachusetts Bay Colony. *(Library of Congress)*

One of Kerry's grandfathers, James Grant Forbes, was born in Shanghai, China, in 1879. He married Margaret Winthrop in 1906. In 1914, Kerry's mother, Rosemary, one of eleven children, was born.

Rosemary met Richard Kerry right before World War II, while living with her family in northern France. Kerry was studying to become a sculptor. Richard and Rosemary married in January 1941, after they both had returned to the United States to escape the war. They traveled separately and Rosemary had only narrowly escaped the German invasion of France in June 1940.

Kerry's mother, Rosemary Forbes Kerry. *(AP Photo / Courtesy of John Kerry.)*

Richard Kerry's background was much less privileged than his new wife's. The surname Kerry suggested an Irish background, and Richard probably thought of himself as Irish-Catholic. He was raised Catholic. But apparently his father had wanted to conceal their true ancestry. John Kerry learned the full details of this background only in early 2003, from the *Boston Globe,* the leading newspaper in Boston. Reporters produced a series of biographical articles on Kerry in preparation for his run for president and had uncovered what they described as "astonishing results."

What the paper discovered was that before he left his home in Vienna, then the capital of the Austrian-Hungarian Empire, Kerry's grandfather, Frederick Kerry, had been born Fritz Kohn. Kohn was Jewish, as was his wife. The couple converted to Catholicism in 1900, as did thousands of other Jews during that era. The rise of the virulent political anti-Semitism that culminated in Nazi-led attempts to obliterate the European Jews had begun early in the twentieth century. The mayor of Vienna was one of the Europe's most vocal anti-Semites. Fearful of the political climate, Kohn changed the family name to Kerry, and he and his wife both were baptized as Catholics.

In 1905, the Kerrys, along with their young son Eric, immigrated to the United States and soon had a daughter, Mildred. They first settled in Chicago, where Frederick did well as a business consultant. In 1915, they moved to Brookline, Massachusetts, a well-to-do suburb of Boston. Their third child, Richard, was born that year. Frederick found success as a shoe merchant. The family owned a Cadillac, even then a luxury car, and was able to travel to Europe.

By 1920, things had changed financially for the Kerry family. Their house had been sold and they had moved to an apartment. Then, on November 23, 1921, about 11:30 in the morning, Frederick headed to the Copley Plaza Hotel, not far from his office. This luxury hotel, built in 1912, still exists today. Frederick went to the men's washroom, pulled a gun from his pocket, and, despite the efforts of some other men in the washroom to stop him, shot himself in the head. He did not leave a suicide note.

Frederick Kerry's death made front-page headlines in several Boston papers. Causes for the suicide were the subject of much speculation, but no one had an answer. One of Frederick's granddaughters later said she had been told the cause: "He had made three fortunes and when he had lost the third fortune, he couldn't face it anymore."

Frederick's estate was small; his granddaughter was probably correct. Still, there was enough family money left to send Richard to Yale University and then Harvard Law School. Afterward, while studying art in France, he met the much wealthier Rosemary Forbes.

Rosemary and Richard welcomed their first child, Margaret, in 1941. On December 11, 1943, their first son, John, was born while the family was stationed with Richard in Denver, Colorado. Richard was serving in the United States Army Air Force. Richard was also being treated for tuberculosis, a very serious lung disease, which kept him out of combat during World War II. He spent the war testing airplanes. (Until 1947, the Air Force was part of the United States Army.)

After his discharge at the end of the war, Richard went to work for a Boston law firm. When John was about four years old, in 1947, the family visited the Forbes home in France, which Rosemary had left in 1940 just steps ahead of the advancing German army. The house was almost a total wreck, with only a stair-

Richard Kerry while serving in the Army Air Force. *(AP Photo / Courtesy of John Kerry.)*

case and a chimney remaining. The Germans had destroyed it in 1944 to keep it from being used by the Allies after the June 1944 D-Day invasion.

The ruins made a strong impression on John. He has called it his earliest memory, a vivid example of war's destruction: "I remember . . . the staircase in the sky, the glass under my feet and my mother was crying." The Forbes family decided to rebuild the house, and it is still a family vacation home.

In 1950, Richard Kerry took a job as a lawyer with the Navy Department in Washington, D.C. About a year

This photograph of the Forbes estate in Saint Briac, France, was taken in 1940, before it was partly burned during World War II. *(AP Photo)*

later, Richard got a new job with the United Nations Bureau at the State Department. The United Nations Bureau handled the legal and political details of the relationship between the United States government and the United Nations.

The family, which now included another daughter, Diana, born in 1947, and son, Cameron, born in 1950, first lived in a townhouse just north of the Potomac River. The house was not big enough, so they moved to a larger house in the Maryland suburb of Chevy Chase.

Political discussions were an important part of family life. The family was particularly excited by the 1952 election of a new senator from Massachusetts. John's younger brother, Cameron, later commented that politics "was all part of the dinner table conversation growing up in Washington—father in government service, paying close attention to presidential elections, and along came John F. Kennedy, a Catholic from Massachusetts, [and a Democrat], with the same initials; all of these things resonated. . . . I think this is really when John began to be actively interested in politics." Kennedy was the first (and still the only) Catholic elected president. That, combined with his unprecedented youth, handsome family, and privileged background, made him a charismatic figure for many Americans.

Politics was one way John Kerry could connect with his father. Richard could be distant at times, perhaps because he lost his own father at a young age. Frederick Kerry's suicide was rarely mentioned in the family, but John always sensed its effect on Richard: "My dad was sort of painfully remote and shut off and angry about . . . the lack of a father." He later added, "I always sensed in my dad a sort of profound sadness." His sister Diana, when asked about Frederick Kerry's impact on the family, responded, "We didn't really go there."

Asked about John Kerry's own reticence to share details about his life, his brother Cameron responded, "The reticence, or whatever, came from both our parents, but from my mother most of all. She was vehement about civic duty. Once, when I started talking about winning a ski race, she said to me 'Shrink it down'— meaning my head. That was one of her expressions."

Modesty and a sense of service ran in the family. Richard, who died in 2001, had been motivated by idealism to go into public service. As a well-trained and talented attorney he could have concentrated on making a great deal of money instead of accepting the relatively modest salary of a foreign service worker.

In 2002, after his father's death, John Kerry reflected on the path of Richard's career: "He went into the State Department thinking they were officers who could change the world, and instead found a bureaucracy. They'd write great memos and no one would read them and nobody would do anything. Finally, he got so exasperated about always being questioned from high up that he wrote his book *The Star-Spangled Mirror.* I think it fair to say that he left the Foreign Service a little bit disillusioned and disappointed by it."

Though World War II had ended in 1945, the world had slipped into a Cold War between the capitalist countries gathered around the United States and the Communist countries primarily influenced by the Soviet Union and, after 1948, the People's Republic of China. The period was called a cold war because there was little actual conflict but a constant fear of a possible war.

The Soviet Union had moved to strengthen its hold on Eastern Europe as soon as World War II was over. Claiming a need to create a buffer of states to protect against another German invasion, Soviet leader Joseph Stalin used his army to seize control of Hungary, Poland, Czechoslovakia, and other parts of Eastern and central Europe. To appease the two victorious parties, Germany was divided into a Communist state in the east and a capitalist state in the west. The world was now aligned in two well-armed camps.

Richard opposed the general approach of the Dwight D. Eisenhower administration. He felt that Eisenhower, who took office in January 1952, concentrated too much on "hard power," relying on the use—or threat—of force for the United States to get its way.

The American government, according to Richard, spent too much time promoting the American form of democracy, regardless of how appropriate this might be for different areas of the world. Richard wanted to concentrate on the rebuilding of Europe and the development of treaties with the European nations that came to make up the North Atlantic Treaty Organization (NATO). Richard thought the Marshall Plan, which made cheap loans available to nations rebuilding after World War II, should have been the first step in a series of cooperative efforts. The Marshall Plan was very successful, and by 1954, the economic recovery of Europe was well underway. He thought it should be expanded and that the United States should work with more international organizations.

Richard eventually presented his ideas in a book published in 1990, *The Star-Spangled Mirror.* The first paragraph of the preface is Richard's first political statement in the book:

> This book is the result of what began as an effort to understand some of the more perplexing peculiarities of American behavior in dealing with our NATO allies. On occasion we seemed to be telling them that we understood their vital interests better than they

did. Persistent efforts to get them to accept ideas of military organization or policies they had no intention of agreeing to only succeeded in exacerbating differences. On many occasions the need to consult them in advance before taking unilateral action was simply ignored, and we often showed visible impatience with consultation.

A few paragraphs later, Richard writes, "The observation that Americans are inclined to see the world and foreign affairs in black and white has become so commonplace as to risk being trite."

Richard joined the American diplomatic service, the Foreign Service, in 1954. He became the legal advisor to the United States representative in Berlin. At the time, Berlin was controlled by a High Commission made up of representatives from the four major nations that had defeated Germany in World War II—the United States, the Soviet Union, Great Britain, and France. Because Berlin was located inside the territory occupied by the Soviets, the city had been split into zones of occupation. Richard's job was to advise the American authorities on the potential legal problems presented by a divided city.

One of these problems was caused by people crossing the border from the western part of Berlin into the eastern part of the city. Not long after the Kerry family's arrival, John went for a bike ride into East Berlin. Crossing from West Berlin (under the control of the United States, France, and Great Britain) into East Berlin was

John Kerry with his siblings. From left: Cameron, Diana, and, right, Peggy. *(AP Photo / Courtesy of John Kerry.)*

illegal. Soviet authorities might have arrested him. This escapade helped Richard and Rosemary decide to send John to boarding school in Switzerland for the next two years.

Kerry was one of three Americans in a school with fifty German students and 150 Italian students. "Those kids could be tough," Kerry later commented, without going into details. It was an unfamiliar and sometimes uncomfortable environment, and Kerry responded by doing better work than the other students. A note once sent home to his mother by the school said of Kerry, "He has developed a rather excessive amount of self-confidence and we find it necessary to take a gentle repressive measure from time to time."

Two years later, John Kerry returned to the United States to attend another boarding school. The remainder of his education, until he went to Yale University, would be at boarding schools. Kerry later recalled, "My parents were fabulous and loving and caring and supportive, but they weren't always around. . . . I was always moving on and saying goodbye. It kind of had an effect on you; it steeled you. There wasn't a lot of permanence and roots. For kids [that's] not the greatest thing."

Richard accepted help from one of his wife's aunts, Clara Winthrop, to pay the boarding school tuition. Clara had no children of her own. Kerry has been quoted as saying that this "was a great and sweet and nice thing from an aunt who had no place" to put her money.

John entered Fessenden School in Massachusetts in 1957. The most notable thing he took from this school was meeting Richard Pershing, grandson of General John J. Pershing, commander of American troops during World War I. Kerry and Pershing became close friends. Though they went to different schools after Fessenden, they would reconnect at Yale. Richard's father was a highly successful stockbroker in New York City.

Fessenden did not have a high school so in 1958 Kerry entered St. Paul's School in Concord, New Hampshire. St. Paul's was founded in 1856 by the Episcopalian Church, and required all boys to attend chapel every day. No other religious facilities were available on campus. A Catholic like Kerry, who wished to attend Catholic mass, had to go into the town of Concord to do so.

Kerry's previous education had prepared him for the tough academics at St. Paul's. High school was more significant for Kerry in social and other nonacademic aspects. He grew to his current height of six feet four inches, and was one of the tallest boys at the school. He played hockey, soccer, and lacrosse. There were other students at St. Paul's who went on to public service, including Robert Mueller, who would become the director of the Federal Bureau of Investigation.

Kerry left a good impression on some people he met at St.

Kerry *(right)* with fellow members of the debate team, from the 1962 St. Paul's yearbook. *(St. Paul's School)*

Paul's. His English teacher, Herbert Church, later recalled, "I thought this was a man who might go somewhere. The thing that impressed me always was his very serious idealism. A lot of guys wanted to be head of Daddy's Wall Street firm, nothing wrong with that, but this young guy, you had a feeling he would do something for the world."

One of Kerry's interests at school was debate. This interest arose from dinner table discussions with his father when he was younger. Kerry took a course at St. Paul's that analyzed the great debates of the past and became a good debater on his own. His St. Paul's classmate Danny Barbiero remembers, "He has always been a very studied person when it comes to his public speaking."

One of his teachers later said that during a formal debate, Kerry seemed "one of the most brilliant people I've ever known." Formal debating requires a strong knowledge of the facts on both sides of the issue. It requires being able to weigh the facts and to argue, with equal conviction, both perspectives.

The student body at St. Paul's was very Republican in political orientation, which came as a challenge to Kerry. Most of the boys there came from well-to-do families, most of which supported the Republican candidate for president in 1960, Richard Nixon. The student body held mock presidential elections every four years, where students could vote to express their presidential preference. Kerry gave a formal speech before the student body urging the election of John F. Kennedy, the Democratic presidential nominee. He did not win them over. The last time the student body had not supported the Republican nominee was 1860.

Though Nixon's background was much more humble than the wealthy Kennedy's, he supported policies much more favorable to the well off. Kennedy's religion was also a factor. Though this fear was rarely stated publicly, some Americans worried that Kennedy would take instructions from the Pope in Rome. Kennedy was finally able to deal with this issue by making a forthright speech about his dedication to the separation of church and state. He scored a victory over Nixon and, in 1961, became president of the United States.

Although she was a committed Democrat, Kerry's mother came from the same social class as most of his fellow students at St. Paul's—but there was little money to go with her prestigious name. Kerry later explained: "We were comfortable. My mother had independent money but by St. Paul's standards I would never have called myself rich. I didn't have to work, in terms of parental support. But my parents were good parents in that they taught me the value of labor . . . I wanted to do it myself. I wanted to make my own way."

At St. Paul's, it was considered unseemly for a boy from the upper class to be openly ambitious. St. Paul's students assumed a good future was due them. The accepted mode of comportment resembled a sense of entitlement; everything should come easy, and one should not try too hard, or at least not seem to try too hard. But Kerry was driven, much like his hero John Kennedy. Kerry was a serious student, somewhat reserved, who did not make friends easily. A teenager who impresses a teacher as serious may come across to his fellow students as strange or arrogant. Yet Kerry didn't waste much time trying to fit in. He always seemed to realize that the primary purpose of high school was to prepare for college. He did well enough academically at St. Paul's to be admitted to Yale University in the fall of 1962.

During the summer between college and high school, Kerry worked briefly for the first Senate campaign of Edward Kennedy, President Kennedy's brother, but neither man remembered meeting then. He also began to

Kerry *(far left)* aboard the Coast Guard yacht *Manitou* with President John F. Kennedy off Narragansett, Rhode Island, on August 26, 1962.

date Janet Auchincloss, the half sister of Jackie Kennedy. One of his roommates had introduced them.

In August 1962, Janet invited Kerry to her family's huge estate in Rhode Island when President Kennedy was visiting. Kerry arrived a bit late for the date, and was directed into the house: "This guy is standing there, he turns around, and it is the President of the United States . . . I remember distinctly saying 'Hi, Mr. Kennedy,' and we chatted. He said, 'Oh, what are you doing?' I said 'I just graduated from St. Paul's. I am about to go to Yale.' He was incredibly warm, incredibly friendly, just relaxed."

Kerry met John Kennedy again a few weeks later at the America's Cup yacht races off of the coast of Rhode Island. President Kennedy was a national hero, and being around him profoundly influenced John Kerry. He headed off for Yale filled with a sense of possibility.

Chapter Two

Yale

John Kerry was not the first member of the Kerry family to attend Yale. Richard Kerry graduated from the prestigious university in 1937. Having a family legacy probably helped to smooth John Kerry's admission. Founded in 1701, Yale was still all male when Kerry entered.

Kerry continued to debate at Yale. He took a course that studied the great debates of the past. "John loved the class," his St. Paul's classmate and Yale roommate, Danny Barbiero, remembered. He was elected president of the Yale Political Union, a prominent debating club, in his junior year. Kerry was more popular at Yale than he had been at St. Paul's.

William "Chip" Stanberry, Kerry's debate partner for three years, was later asked what he thought drove Kerry at Yale. He answered, "John would clearly say, 'If I could make my dream come true, it would be running for president of the United States.' It was not a casual interest. It was a serious, stated interest. His lifelong ambition was to be in political office . . . I don't think there was any one specific issue . . . I don't think he had pet issues as much as he simply said, 'The life of a politician is the life I want. I want to speak out on issues. This is what I want to do for a job.'" Kerry combined his ambition with a general desire to do good.

Kerry played varsity soccer at Yale. His most memorable soccer game, however, had nothing to do with athletics. The soccer team played on Fridays. Of Friday, November 22, 1963, Kerry later said, "I remember the ripple going through the crowd and wondering what was going on because people were clearly distracted from the game. And then we heard the President had been shot in Dallas. Somehow we played the game and to this day I can't tell you who won." Americans everywhere were shocked at the news their beloved president had been assassinated.

Kerry on the Yale hockey team. *(AP Photo)*

Kerry was very upset about the murder of his hero. His roommates noted that he spent the next few days just staring, numb, at the television. Millions of Americans did the same thing. His cousin Serita Winthrop drove up from New York City to New Haven to be with him. She finally persuaded him to take a walk with her. "We were walking around the campus at Yale University and he talked at length about how much he admired Kennedy . . . He had so clearly invested in the President. It was more than just sharing the same initials—it was as if a family member had been killed."

Kerry later agreed: "It was a huge stunner to me. Just really pulled the rug out from under me . . . It sort of robbed us of our moment, our youth, all the enthusiasm we had for a while." Kerry's comment reflects the attitude of many people alive at the time. Kennedy was about thirty years younger than the president he replaced, Dwight D. Eisenhower, and he had brought a more vibrant and vigorous energy to the presidency. His death cast a shadow over the country that his vice president, Lyndon B. Johnson, would be unable to lift.

Kerry's career at Yale was about more than academics. He later recalled, "I was a capable student, but not a very dedicated one." One course he did enjoy was on American diplomacy, taught by Professor Gaddis Smith, a specialist on World War II and the Cold War.

Smith seems to have met the first requirement of a good teacher. He made his subject come alive and captured the students' interest. Kerry remembered Smith "was a great, great lecturer. The lectures were all full of energy and knowledge." Smith did not work from text-books, preferring to hand out mimeographed copies of primary-source documents. He would then deliver vivid, dynamic lectures on the particular topics.

The Vietnam War was a major topic in Smith's class. Smith tried to present all sides of the issue that he said had roots stretching back a hundred years. For decades, Vietnam had been controlled by France, which wanted access to such natural resources as rubber and oil. After World War II, a militia force called the Viet Minh, led by an expatriate who had taken the name Ho Chi Minh, resisted French control. In 1954, the French suffered a stunning and crippling defeat in the long battle of Dienbienphu. French domination of Vietnam was over. During the peace negotiations, the country was divided into North and South Vietnam. The north was under the control of Ho Chi Minh, who established a Communist government. The south was anti-Communist and asked the U.S. for support. Elections intended to unify the country were supposed to be held after the peace agree-ment, but the leaders of South Vietnam, supported by American advisors, refused to hold the elections.

South Vietnam did hold a local election in 1956, which brought to power a staunch anti-Communist, Ngo Dinh Diem. Communist guerrillas inside the South, who came to be called the Viet Cong, as well as army forces from the North, began making attacks on the South.

President John Kennedy had vastly increased the number of American military advisors to South Viet-nam from a few hundred when he took office in 1961 to

This map shows Vietnam in the early 1960s, with a line indicating the demarcation between the north and the south.

about 16,000 by the time he was assassinated. An incident in the Gulf of Tonkin, in which the North Vietnamese were said to have attacked American ships without provocation, led the U.S. Congress to pass the Tonkin Gulf resolution. It authorized the president to use force if he believed it to be necessary. Johnson began sending in troops by the thousands. The Vietnam War, which was to play such a large part in Kerry's life and career, was raging by time he enrolled in Professor Smith's class. Active opposition to the war at home, however, was not yet widespread.

Smith, an opponent to the war, tried to present to his students all views and all shades within these positions. Smith remembered, "I tried to offer a full spectrum of opinions on Vietnam." This ran from full support to the "arrogance of power" argument made by some opponents—the idea that a powerful nation, such as the United States, should resist the temptation to throw its weight around. The United States should try to persuade, not force, other nations to go along with what it might want. Smith argued that the biggest problem in Vietnam was ignorance of Asian culture; the United States government did not understand the politics and culture of the region.

The basic goal of Smith's class was to make his students think, not necessarily to get them to accept his positions. Kerry and other students were encouraged to ask questions. Their answers and their conclusions should be their own. Students spent hours of class time challenging each other's beliefs—and their own.

During his last three years at Yale, Kerry lived in a residential college called Jonathan Edwards College. Yale residential colleges are more than just normal college dorms. They also have libraries and auditoriums, and large, dramatic entrance hallways. Jonathan Edwards College, known informally as JE, had a special fund that was used weekly for concerts or art exhibits. Kerry lived in a three-room suite, made up of two bedrooms and a living room. He liked to stay up late, so his suitemates, Danny Barbiero and Harvey Bundy, let him have a bedroom for himself while they shared a room.

Kerry's JE experience had at least one effect on his life. His roommate Harvey Bundy was the nephew of both William and McGeorge Bundy, each a foreign policy expert working for the Johnson administration. William Bundy, then assistant secretary of state for Far Eastern affairs, came to the Yale campus to speak in support of the Vietnam War. After one speech, Bundy visited his nephew's suite and spoke with the suitemates. He stressed the importance of the effort in Vietnam in defending American interests and resisting communism. He urged the three Yale students to become military officers and to go to Vietnam to help lead the efforts. Barbiero later said, "I don't know that he was the prime mover in us going, but he certainly was an influence. He was an assistant secretary of state."

In his senior year, Kerry became one of the fifteen members inducted into Skull and Bones. This is an exclusive club for Yale students "destined to do great things—or at least for those who were or sought to be well connected." The outgoing members elect fifteen new members finishing their junior year.

Because Skull and Bones is a secret society, it is not easy to find reliable information about it. As a result, rumors and legends abound. Most reports indicate that it is not a secret cabal intent on controlling the government, but a small, elite social club and a base for current and future networking. Membership in the society is a bond that members share the rest of their lives.

Kerry's Yale debating partner, Chip Stanberry, said they did not really become close friends until their

JOHN FORBES KERRY. Born December 11, 1943, in Denver, Colorado, son of Richard John Kerry, '37, and Rosemary Forbes Kerry. Prepared at St. Paul's School, Concord, N. H. Entered Yale, September, 1962. Political Science Major; won Parker Dickson Buck-Schuyler B. Jackson Prize (oratory), 1964, Henry James Teneyck Prize (oratory), 1965, and Thacher Memorial Debating Contest, 1964 and 1965. Member: Jonathan Edwards (College Advisory Board, 1962-65; soccer, 1962); Fence Club; Haunt Club; Pundits; Skull and Bones; Political Union, 1962-66, president, 1964-65; Liberal Party, 1962-66, chairman, 1963-64; Yale Debating Association, 1962-66; Yale Young Democrats, 1962-63, treasurer, 1962-63; Conn. Intercollegiate State Legislature, 1962-65, treasurer, 1963-64; Yale Young Republicans, 1965-66; Freshman hockey (numerals); J. V. hockey, 1963-66; J. V. lacrosse, 1966; Varsity soccer, 1963-65 (major "Y", 1965). Roommates: H. H. Bundy III, D. P. Barbiero. Future study: law. Address: Indian Hill Road, Groton, Mass.

Entry from the 1966 Yale yearbook. *(Yale University)*

membership the same year in Skull and Bones. Stanberry said, "We think of politicians as garrulous and backslapping. John was private and reserved. He was shy to jump into a crowded circle of four guys having a beer. People therefore mistook him as aloof. [Within Skull and Bones, however, Kerry was] relaxed, he was more natural. He broke out of whatever that shy, reserved part of his person was. John took it seriously, and it means a lot to him. Of course, John took everything seriously."

Kerry's closest friends were members of Skull and Bones. Kerry had roomed with Dick Pershing at Fessenden before Kerry went to St. Paul's. Fred Smith, another friend from Skull and Bones, got Kerry interested in learning to fly. Smith wrote a term paper at Yale on the somewhat-esoteric topic of society's need for a new logistics system to support increased automation. The paper barely earned a passing grade, but Smith later used the principals he presented to found Federal Express.

Another close friend at Yale was David Thorne. Without knowing it, he and Kerry both had dated Janet Auchincloss. Thorne had a twin sister, Julia. Kerry met her just before the start of his second year at Yale. Kerry pulled up in his Volkswagen Bus to visit David Thorne at the Thorne family estate on Long Island. Julia was standing in front, wearing a bikini, loudly singing a folk song. "He just kind of stood there and looked," Julia later told an interviewer. The attraction was mutual.

As graduation neared, Yale seniors had to think about the possibility of being drafted to serve in the United States Army. The draft had been in effect continuously since 1948 and was used to fill slots in the army left unfilled by volunteers. During Kerry's college years, from 1962-1966, more than 900,000 men were inducted into the army by the Selective Service System. While this number was small compared to the ten-million-plus inducted during World War II, almost 2,000 of those serving in Vietnam were killed and more than 7,000 wounded.

Many Yale students could use their connections to avoid or delay military service. Graduate school was one way to earn a deferment. The way the system worked allowed the privileged to avoid military service while working-class young men were more likely to be drafted. Of the roughly 27 million men eligible for the draft during the Vietnam War, 15 million obtained deferments.

It was a surprise to many of his classmates when Kerry signed up for the United States Navy in the fall of 1965, during his senior year. Though he was aware of the potential for danger, he was still imbued with the sense of duty he learned from his father and from his hero, John Kennedy. Kerry made plans to enter the navy after graduation, in the spring of 1966.

Kerry, the president of the Yale Political Union debating society, was selected for the honor of giving the class oration at graduation. One line in the original speech, reprinted in the class yearbook—the yearbook went to press before the graduation ceremonies—read: "We need no ringing call to do great things but only a small stimulus to do that which will make a constructive contribution to society—if you will to make this a better world to live in."

A week before graduation, Kerry and the other fourteen members of Skull and Bones went on a vacation trip to a resort island owned by the society. This was a time when the American involvement in Vietnam was becoming a contentious issue. Kerry had a chance to think while on this trip and decided to write a totally new speech.

The new speech read, in part, "We have not really lost the desire to serve. We question the very roots of what we are serving." The first draft was a traditional

Ivy League speech. A recent analysis of Kerry's career and his background concluded that "the speech [Kerry actually] gave, hastily rewritten at the last moment, was anything but traditional: it was a broad, passionate criticism of American foreign policy, including the war that he would soon be fighting." Kerry's friend Fred Smith later commented on the seeming inconsistency of Kerry delivering a speech criticizing American foreign policy after he had joined the navy. Smith said, "Our decisions were all about our sense of duty. We were the Kennedy generation—you know, 'Pay any price, bear any burden.' That was the ethos."

Kerry's friend Danny Barbiero later speculated on another reason Kerry and his friends enlisted despite their doubts about the war: "We have the naïve reasons college kids would have. We thought, let's go and see what's really happening." The *Washington Post* quotes Kerry as having said in 1970 that he joined the navy and went to Vietnam "because he wanted to study that policy first hand." Clearly, the decision to enlist in the military, when it meant he was likely to see combat, was a complex decision with several different motivations.

Yale gave Kerry lifelong friends, particularly David Thorne and Fred Smith, as well as a first-rate education. Debate provided him with skills and experience in examining all sides of an issue, as well as an understanding of the importance of learning as much as possible about an issue. Professor Smith's class refined this need and desire to question and examine all positions, particularly those of the government. All of these experiences would prove to be valuable when put to the test in the crucible that was Vietnam.

Chapter Three

Vietnam

Within a few weeks after graduating Yale in the spring of 1966, Kerry started naval training. He first attended a sixteen-week Officer Candidates School (OCS) training program at Newport, Rhode Island. This was a tough introduction to the military and the navy.

Kerry later joked about how he looked with his newly shaved head: "I was not meant to have no hair. God gave me a strange head shape, and baldness just doesn't work. It's not Bruce Willis's look at all I had. It was an ungainly sight. I was miserable; glad we weren't able to leave the base. Going off base would have riot-shock value: cruel and unusual punishment to gazers."

At the end of 1966, Ensign John Kerry arrived for four months of advanced training in San Francisco, part of what would turn out to be a thirteen-month training process before he deployed for his first tour in Vietnam. As a junior officer (one of the lower-ranking officers), Kerry was being trained in what to do if his ship was

From left to right: David Thorne, John Kerry, and Fred Smith posing on an airplane wing. *(David Thorne)*

attacked and hit. As well as being trained in how to handle damage from conventional explosives, Kerry and his fellow junior officers were trained in how to handle chemical, biological, and nuclear attacks.

His friend David Thorne was training in San Diego, where Kerry was sent for more advanced naval training. One afternoon in the spring of 1967, on a three-day leave, they rented a private plane. Thorne proposed they fly the four hundred miles to San Francisco. As they reached the city, Kerry then decided to fly under the Golden Gate Bridge. This may have been the first step in flying a loop around the bridge. Kerry had previously expressed admiration for the feat.

As the plane approached the bridge, they spotted a sea gull flying near the wing. Kerry and Thorne then heard a loud thump. Apparently another bird had actually hit the wing. The small plane shook as Kerry pulled up to gain altitude. They then noticed they had flown into an entire flock of seagulls. Kerry turned away from the bridge and got permission for an emergency landing at a nearby airport. Thorne later described the experience as "hair raising." Had a bird been sucked into the engine, the plane might well have crashed, perhaps even into the bridge. Kerry's career might have ended with a brief notice of the accident in the back pages of the *San Francisco Chronicle*.

In June 1967, Kerry and Thorne, both in southern California, heard that President Lyndon Johnson was going to speak at a Democratic fund-raiser at the Century Plaza Hotel in Los Angeles. By this time, the United States was involved in major combat in Vietnam. The total number of Americans killed in Vietnam had reached 19,000 by the end of 1967. Fewer than 2,000 Americans were killed in Vietnam through 1965, 6,000 in 1966, and 11,000 in 1967.

Kerry and Thorne obtained leave and went to watch the crowds of protestors gathered outside the hotel. A crowd of 15,000 walked by noisily chanting, "Hey, hey, LBJ, how many kids did you kill today?" Many of the protestors halted in front of the hotel but remained peaceful according to Kerry and Thorne. Los Angeles had assigned 1,300 police officers, probably about a third of its entire police force at the time, to protect the hotel. The cops cracked down, arresting fifty-one people on the grounds of unlawful assembly or refusal to disperse. Thorne remembered, "It seemed like a perfectly

In 1967, antiwar protests, such as the one Kerry and Thorne attended in Los Angeles, were taking place across the country. This demonstration in front of the UN happened on April 15, 1967. *(AP Photo)*

peaceful thing, and then the police got aggressive, started whacking people." Kerry and Thorne thought the police overreacted. The Vietnam War was becoming a divisive domestic political issue as well as a foreign policy question.

Later that month, not long after he and David Thorne witnessed the Los Angeles demonstration, Kerry was assigned to duty aboard the guided missile frigate USS *Gridley*. A guided missile frigate is a relatively small warship usually used for fire support against land or sea targets. Kerry served on this vessel for a year. Little of note occurred during this year of service.

Kerry's regular duties on the ship were not glamorous. As he later put it, "I was responsible for what is called First Division, which is all the deck work: over-

```
                                                    10 February 1968

From:  Ensign John F. KERRY, ████████
To:    Chief of Naval Personnel (Pers-B14)
Via:   Commanding Officer, USS GRIDLEY (DLG-21)

Subj:  Vietnam Duty; request for

1.  I request duty in Vietnam. My billet preference is "Swift" boats
    with a second choice of Patrol Officer in a PBR Squadron.
```

An excerpt from a letter Kerry sent to his commanding officer on February 10, 1968. The first line reads, "I request duty in Vietnam."

seeing all seamen on the ship, the appearance of the vessel . . . Then when you get out to sea, you're the guys who are manning the line and anchor. You're responsible for the seagoing components." "Seagoing components" differentiates these functions from the weaponry of the ship, which included missiles and cannon.

Naval ships alternate between deployment overseas and service in American waters. In early 1968, the *Gridley* was on its way across the Pacific to Asia when the war suddenly became personal for Kerry.

The Tet Offensive was a massive North Vietnamese and Viet Cong assault timed to occur during the Vietnamese New Year, or Tet, celebrated at the end of January 1968. The American military and the American political leaders had been assuring the public that the war was going very well for the United States, that American leaders could see the light at the end of the tunnel. Then, suddenly, the Communists, supposedly on the verge of defeat, attacked cities and military bases all over Vietnam, most notably in Hue, South Vietnam's second largest city, and in the capital, Saigon. Most embarrassingly for the United States, North Vietnamese troops were even able to enter the American embassy compound.

Militarily, all the attacks were fought off and the North Vietnamese/Viet Cong effort failed. General William Westmoreland, commander of all American troops in Vietnam, was basically right, though he got the numbers wrong when, on the day the American embassy had been attacked, he told the press, "Some superficial damage has been done to the buildings, the nineteen Vietcong who entered have been killed. American troops have gone on the offensive and are pursuing the enemy aggressively."

He might have been almost right, but Westmoreland missed the point. Tet proved to be a major political defeat. Government assurances of pending success, issued regularly since the dispatch of American combat troops to Vietnam in early 1965, had been shown to be clearly inaccurate. Victory, if it was coming at all, was far in the future.

Kerry's close friend Dick Pershing was already in Vietnam during the Tet Offensive. He served as a second lieutenant and commanded a platoon that was rushed into action at the end of January 1968 to help fight off the Tet attacks. In the fight, Pershing's platoon lost about half its strength. Two weeks later, Pershing and his men were on patrol in a rice paddy when the Viet Cong launched a surprise attack. After the firefight was over, Pershing noticed one of his men was missing. While looking for the man or his remains, Pershing was killed.

Kerry was aboard the *Gridley* headed to Vietnamese waters when he received a telegram informing him that his close friend had been killed. He was badly shaken. Too far at sea to attend the funeral, he poured out his feelings in a letter to his parents. Kerry described himself as "empty, bitter, angry and desperately lost with nothing but war, violence and more war around me. I just don't believe it was meant to be this cruel and senseless."

The *Gridley* was headed to the Gulf of Tonkin, the body of water off the coast of Vietnam. Its job was to

This 1968 map of Vietnam shows the Gulf of Tonkin, where Kerry served during his first tour.

help protect the aircraft carrier *Kitty Hawk.* Most of the military power of an aircraft carrier to attack and to defend itself comes from its airplanes. Carriers need smaller ships to defend them against attack from other ships. The *Gridley* patrolled the gulf for several weeks. Kerry saw no combat duty while on board.

When his ship returned to California in June 1968, Kerry was met by David Thorne and his sister Julia They brought the bad news that Robert Kennedy, running for the Democratic nomination for president, had been assassinated. Kerry, and many other Americans, had seen the election of Robert Kennedy as the best way to end the war. His assassination came just two months after the civil rights leader Martin Luther King Jr. had been murdered. Kerry thought that if the country was not actually falling apart, as it seemed to many people, it certainly was in deep trouble. Julia later recalled, "It was awful. We were in shock."

After his leave, Kerry volunteered for service in what were called swift boats. For the first years of the American involvement in Vietnam, the United States Navy patrolled out to sea. They call this "blue water," for the open ocean. Then, in 1966, the navy began to expand its role in Vietnam. The Mekong Delta, the place where several branches of the large Mekong River meet the sea, covers a large section of South Vietnam. The North Vietnamese and the Viet Cong took full advantage of the delta and the other rivers and canals common to the countryside to infiltrate men and supplies into the South.

The navy decided to do something about the problem, which required engaging in extensive "brown water" or "riverine" operations for the first time since the American Civil War. Swift boats, known to the navy as "patrol craft, fast" or "PCF," were added to the fleet. Their basic role was to sail up rivers, even narrow canals, to look for Viet Cong and to try to draw fire from the enemy hidden in the jungles on shore.

The swift boats had to be adapted to this new, unanticipated use. These were small craft with aluminum hulls, roughly fifty feet long. Their shallow draft—the amount of the ship below the water line—made them able to operate in relatively shallow rivers and canals. Swift boats, however, were not equipped for military use. They were not armored, having been designed as water taxis to take crew and supplies to offshore oil platforms. In Vietnam the crews would improvise pro-

A swift boat, or "PCF."

tection by hanging flak jackets, usually worn by individuals, over the sides of the boat. Commanding a swift boat was a dangerous mission. John Kerry volunteered for the duty.

But before he returned to Vietnam, Kerry and Julia Thorne became engaged. They told only their family and close friends.

Kerry arrived back in Vietnam in November 1968. He spent two weeks on routine coastal patrol before volunteering for a mission. On the night of December 2, 1968, Kerry and two enlisted sailors went on a night patrol on a small boat to search for Viet Cong. They were in what was known as a free-fire zone, with a nighttime curfew. Anyone violating the curfew could be considered the enemy and shot.

A few hours into the mission, Kerry and his two associates got into a firefight with several sampans, or small boats. Kerry was hit in the arm by a piece of shrapnel, a fragment of metal. Kerry had begun keeping a journal while in Vietnam, writing down his experiences and impressions. Sections of the journal have been published in a history of Kerry's experiences in Vietnam. He wrote of this incident: "We opened fire. The light from the flares [which the Americans had fired to enable themselves to get a better view of their targets] started to fade, the air was full of explosions. My M-16 [the standard automatic rifle for American military in Vietnam] jammed, and as I bent down, a stinging piece of heat socked into my arm and just seemed to burn like hell. . . . I felt terribly seasoned after this minor skirmish, but since I couldn't put my finger on what we have really accomplished or what had happened, it was difficult to feel satisfied."

The wound was not life threatening but required a doctor to remove the piece of shrapnel. Kerry was awarded the Purple Heart, a medal given to anyone wounded in the service of the United States when the wound requires medical attention.

In the second week of December 1968, Kerry was given the command of a swift boat: PCF 44. Kerry and his five sailors had an average age of nineteen. PCF carried three machine guns plus additional small arms.

Kerry's first action in this new boat came on December 24, 1968. A truce, an agreement between the sides to temporarily stop fighting, had been agreed to for that evening, but in Kerry's area, near the border between Vietnam and Cambodia, the truce fell apart almost immediately. Enemy fire exploded around PCF 44, on patrol with several other boats. "Where is the enemy?" one member of the crew shouted during the fighting. Some distance away, but visible from the boat, an elderly Vietnamese man, apparently tending his water buffalo, was actually serving as a human shield for twelve Viet Cong manning a machine gun nest.

Kerry ordered his men to open fire. One of the men, with an M-60 machine gun, shot and killed the old man, who fell into the water. Kerry's crew was then able to silence the enemy machine gun.

The same night, some South Vietnamese began firing into the river without checking to see if anyone was there. Kerry's boat was almost hit as it headed back to base. Soon after, Kerry described the battle in his journal: "Suddenly, in a flash, there is a moment of hell and blindness, the reeds erupt and bullets walk out across the water at your boat and those around you. . . . From PBR and Swift a cacophony of explosions as they answer with shame, anger, and surprise the wall of fire that met them. Quickly . . . you are past the ambush point and you wheel your boats around to run back and out into the main river. From somewhere reason calls you and you grab the loudspeaker and yell to your men to hold your fire [to increase chances of hitting a target] until right on top of the spot."

Near the end of January 1969, Kerry was transferred to the command of PCF 94, whose captain had been wounded. PCF 44 was being repaired and its crew was transferred to others areas. Back in the U.S., President Lyndon Johnson had not run for reelection in 1968. Republican Richard Nixon was elected due in great part to his promise to pursue negotiations with the North Vietnamese to end the war.

But peace was a long way off. Nixon decided to increase military force to try to convince the North Vietnamese to negotiate a settlement. Kerry suddenly found himself to be very busy. In two months, he saw sufficient action to win two more Purple Hearts and two medals for gallantry under fire: the Bronze Star and the Silver Star.

On February 20, 1969, PCF 94 and another PCF were on river patrol. They spotted three men in black, the uniform of the Viet Cong, running along a riverbank. The Americans opened fire, and the Viet Cong fired back. Kerry took shrapnel in the thigh and earned his second Purple Heart. A navy report on the incident noted that the PCFs had destroyed forty sampans, ten huts, three bunkers, and 5,000 pounds of rice.

Kerry and his crew saw action several more times in the next two weeks. On February 28, 1969, Kerry got word that another swift boat was being ambushed. As his boat raced to the scene, PCF 94 had a window broken by a Viet Cong B-40 rocket grenade. Rocket grenades are explosive charges shot out of a gun-like device that a single man can carry. They could be used against many different types of targets, but were usually used against vehicles and boats. The normal procedure would have been to shoot back at the enemy and then withdraw. Kerry tried something different, turning his boat towards the riverbank to provide a narrower target while firing, and then ordering the boat to be beached so his men could chase the enemy on land.

As the boat scraped ashore, a teenager carrying a grenade launcher appeared out of the bush. The guerrilla had a weapon that could have badly damaged or destroyed Kerry's boat. However, as Kerry later put it, "we were literally face to face . . . and he didn't pull the trigger."

Another member of the crew, Frederick Short, who was sitting in a gun turret—more a tub than an armored emplacement—later said he thought the Viet Cong teenager did not fire because he knew he was too close to the boat. He would have been injured or killed himself by the explosion. Short was unable to initially fire at the guerrilla because with the boat beached, the walls of the tub prevented him from angling his guns to reach nearby targets on the ground.

PCF 94's forward gunner fired at the Viet Cong, grazing him in the leg. Then the gun jammed. When the guerrilla got up and started to run, Kerry realized they had to get him before he took shelter behind a hut and was able to fire a grenade. Kerry chased the guerrilla behind the hut and shot and killed him. Short was able to give Kerry covering fire—aiming at the nearby woods to force the other enemy in the area to keep undercover. Kerry was awarded the military's second highest honor, the Silver Star, for this action.

Kerry won a second medal, the Bronze Star, two weeks later, and a third Purple Heart. A mine went off

Lieutenant Kerry being awarded the Bronze Star.

near Kerry's boat, wounding him in the right arm. The boat was being shot at from both banks. Despite his wound, Kerry was able to rescue a soldier, Jim Rasmussen, who had been thrown overboard.

Kerry had been wounded three times, and three Purple Hearts, under naval rules then in effect, enabled any sailor the right to request a return home immediately. Kerry applied for and was granted a transfer to duty as an admiral's aide in Brooklyn, New York. Before he left, Kerry arranged for all members of the crew of PFC 94 to transfer to safer assignments within Vietnam.

Despite his objections to U.S. involvement in the war, Kerry did his best when he got to Vietnam. He performed bravely and his commanding officers reported that he showed imagination and decisive leadership. But when Kerry left Vietnam he was more an opponent of the war than he had been before. Prior to his service, he had disagreed with U.S. policy, but after seeing the death and suffering that policy was causing, he was now committed to doing what he could to get the U.S. out of Vietnam.

Chapter Four

Vietnam Veterans Against the War

Thirty years after leaving Vietnam, Kerry spoke to a reporter about what was going through his mind as he left: "I thought it was time to tell the story of what was happening over there. I was angry about what happened over there, I had clearly concluded how wrong it was."

Kerry had tried to do his duty in Vietnam, and he sensed that most people around him were doing the same. When he returned he was convinced that his and his fellow soldiers' efforts and lives were being wasted. He had always wanted a career in public service. Convincing Americans and their leaders that it was time to get out of the war seemed to be a good place to start that career.

When he returned to the United States, Kerry saw that Vietnam veterans were not being welcomed home as heroes. They were lucky if they could quietly return and readjust to civilian life. Kerry believed this was an injustice that needed to be addressed. During this time, however, Kerry was still an active duty naval officer and could not protest the war while wearing his uniform.

Kerry was actually still in the navy when he made his first connection to the anti-Vietnam War movement. In 1969, his sister Margaret, known as Peggy, was working in the offices of a Vietnam War protest group in New York. Adam Walinsky, a former Robert F. Kennedy aide and speechwriter, needed someone to fly him around New York state in a small plane so he could speak at antiwar rallies. Peggy volunteered her brother.

Kerry flew Walinsky to the rallies. Kerry was not in uniform and he did not speak at the events. On January 3, 1970, Kerry asked for early discharge from the navy. The request was granted, and Kerry found himself a civilian six months before he expected.

Kerry decided to seek the Democratic nomination for the Third Congressional District in eastern Massachusetts. A "citizen's caucus" met on February 22, 1970, to select an antiwar Democrat to oppose the local pro-war Democratic congressman, Philip J. Philbin, in a primary. Philbin was seventy-one at the time. Kerry was twenty-seven. Several other candidates withdrew during the meeting and threw their support to Kerry. But one candidate remained, and when a deadlock looked possible, Kerry threw his support to Father Robert J. Drinan, who went on to win the primary and the general election.

In May of 1970, Kerry married Julia Thorne. The *New York Times* ran a brief story on the wedding, re-

Julia and John on their wedding day, May 23, 1970.

porting, "Miss Julia Stimson Thorne, whose ancestors helped to shape the American republic in its early days, and John Forbes Kerry, who wants to steer it back from what he considers a wayward course, were married . . ."

The start of the anti-Vietnam War movement in the United States cannot be dated exactly. President Johnson sent the first American combat troops in early 1965 and later that year he ordered heavy bombing of North Vietnam, which was aiding the Viet Cong with supplies and manpower. The first major anti-Vietnam War march occurred in Washington, D.C., in November 1965.

The Vietnam War was explained to the American people as necessary to contain—to stop the spread of—communism in the so-called "third world." Initially, the vast majority of the American people supported the war and its goal, and might have continued to support it if they saw success. Instead, what they saw was a series of unstable military dictatorships seizing power in Saigon, the South Vietnamese capital, and the U.S. government repeatedly claiming there was a light at the end of the tunnel, which never seemed to get closer. More and more, the American people realized that Vietnam had become a morass.

With Julia, Kerry became more active in antiwar organizing and protests. In 1970, he joined a group called Vietnam Veterans Against the War (VVAW), which had been founded in New York in 1967. The *New York Times*, in a 1971 article, said that Kerry had been invited to join the group. "While campaigning for Father Drinan, Mr. Kerry appeared on the Dick Cavett television program [a prime-time talk show of the time] and was seen by members of the Vietnam Veterans Against the War, who asked him if he would work for their group. He has been a full-time organizer for them ever since."

The group was not well known at the time. Then, during January 1971, VVAW held hearings in Detroit that they called the "Winter Soldier Investigations," designed to focus American attention on the war.

Kerry did not speak at this meeting, but he suggested the group hold a rally in Washington on the Mall. This rally "was basically my concept," Kerry remembered. "It grew out of my frustration of what I saw in the Winter Soldier effort. Winter Soldier did not break through. . . . I was struck by the lack of interest. America was asleep and the people didn't care. . . . So I suggested a march on Washington." In another interview, Kerry recalled that he "became the unofficial coordinator-organizer."

Some VVAW leaders considered Kerry opportunistic. He had not spoken at the Winter Soldier hearings yet he now seemed to be making himself into a VVAW spokesman. Others, however, realized that Kerry, who was clean shaven with relatively short hair, was far more conventional-looking than many other VVAW leaders and could present a more sympathetic image to the public.

Kerry's own attitude was described in an interview with the *New York Times* in 1971. Kerry described himself at the time as "still a moderate. I'm not a radical in any sense of the word. I guess I'm just an angry young man. . . . If the shores of this country were threatened, I'd be the first to defend it."

President Richard Nixon's administration soon saw Kerry, with his Ivy League education and highly decorated service in Vietnam, as a danger to their efforts to continue the war. In a June 2003 series, the *Boston Globe* wrote, "Nixon aides [and Nixon himself] worried that Kerry was a unique, charismatic leader who could undermine support for the war. Other veteran protesters were easier targets, with their long hair, their use of a Viet Cong flag, and, in some cases, their calls for overthrowing the U.S. government."

Nixon aide Charles Colson, who went to prison for

his part in the Watergate scandal that would destroy the Nixon presidency a few years later, wrote a secret memo outlining how to get at Kerry. It was characteristic of the Nixon administration to try to find damaging information on its opponents that could be used to destroy their reputations. In a line that, ironically, was reflected in the presidential campaign of 2004, Colson described his goal: "Destroy the young demagogue before he becomes another Ralph Nader." During the 1960s and 1970s, Ralph Nader was a noted consumer advocate, particularly famous for exposing dangerous products manufactured by big business.

The Washington protest was set for the week of April 20, 1971. Kerry spent some of this time at the Georgetown townhouse of a friend, working the phones to round up veterans and raise funds.

The first of three major events occurred on April 22. Kerry testified before the Senate Foreign Relations Committee in a televised hearing. The high point of Kerry's testimony was when he posed the poignant rhetorical question, "How do you ask a man to be the last man to die in Vietnam? How do you ask a man to be the last man to die for a mistake?"

Kerry's remarks also summarized what he had heard at the VVAW hearings in Detroit in January 1971. Some of the soldiers in Detroit had confessed to committing serious atrocities while in Vietnam. Although he was repeating what he had heard and not creating the charges, this part of his testimony angered some veterans, including some who had served with Kerry. One

Kerry during his testimony before the Senate Foreign Relations Committee on behalf of the VVAW, April 22, 1971.

fellow swift boat commander later stated that he was "appalled, angry but not surprised. I thought he was behaving like an opportunist."

The next day, April 23, Kerry and the other VVAW members wanted to personally return their military medals to members of Congress. But Capitol Hill was fenced off during the demonstrations, an unfortunate piece of imagery that made it look like Congress was trying to seal itself off from the people.

VVAW leaders decided to throw their medals over a fence into a trash bin. Hundreds of veterans, including Kerry, threw medals and ribbons over the fence. The next day, April 24, 1971, 250,000 people gathered on the Mall. Several such marches occurred during the height of American involvement in Vietnam.

The White House plotting against Kerry continued. However, as Chuck Colson recently admitted, "I don't ever remember finding anything negative about Kerry or hearing anything negative about him. If we had found anything, I'm sure we would have used it to discredit him." The Nixon administration then tried another tactic. They enlisted a swift boat veteran named John O'Neill, who had served in the boats shortly after Kerry left Vietnam and was outraged at Kerry's testimony before the Senate Foreign Relations Committee. The Nixon administration hoped to turn O'Neill into a counterweight to Kerry. O'Neill was even invited to the White House for what turned out to be a one-hour meeting with the president. Colson was particularly interested in arranging a public debate between Kerry and O'Neill. He tried to force Kerry's cooperation by spreading a rumor that Kerry was ducking the confrontation.

Kerry, who was confident in his debating skills, did not have to be convinced to share the stage with O'Neill. The two appeared together on June 30, 1971, on the *Dick Cavett Show*. This was a popular talk show of the day. O'Neill was visibly angry and highly emotional during the program. He started off by accusing Kerry of being "the type of person who lives and survives on the war-weariness and fears of the American people." Kerry maintained a much calmer and more deliberate image. He had a briefing notebook with documentation to back up his case. Kerry wore a dark blue suit while O'Neill showed up in a light suit and white socks.

The message Kerry presented was summed up when he stated that the veterans were not trying to tear down the country. Rather, they were trying to say to the American people, "Here is where we went wrong, and we've got to change. What we say is, the killing can stop tomorrow." Kerry admitted he had not seen

Kerry during his appearance on the *Dick Cavett Show*. *(AP Photo)*

atrocities of the type he had described a few months before at the Senate hearing. But he did cite military operations in which he participated, such as free-fire zones, which allow shooting at anything that moves, which he said were against the laws of war. Kerry showed that he was not afraid to defend his views.

Kerry left the VVAW about a year after he joined. He told a reporter in December 1971 that Nixon "has been very successful in quelling the emotions against the war in this country. He has convinced a lot of people that he is ending it." In reality, American participation in the war would drag on for two more years. Kerry was also opposed to some of the more radical activities of the group, such as burning the American flag. Still, in that one year, Kerry had been an effective leader of the Vietnam Veterans Against the War and the antiwar movement in general.

The antiwar movement did achieve some success. In December 1969, the Nixon administration introduced a draft lottery in an attempt to create a more equitable system. Birth dates were picked at random to determine the order in which young men would be called up. As the war remained unpopular at home and increasingly unwinnable on the ground, Nixon and his advisors began pulling troops out while at the same time stepping up bombing campaigns. Nixon also began to work harder to make the South Vietnamese forces more responsible for their own defense. But in the end, the South was defeated by the combined forces of the Viet Cong and the North Vietnamese army in 1975. The last U.S. troops left and the country was officially reunited under Communist control in 1976. Saigon was renamed Ho Chi Minh City and the war was finally over. American casualties totaled more than 50,000 dead and many more wounded. Nearly one and a half million Vietnamese were killed and countless more lives affected by the war.

Chapter Five

The Years in Exile

In 1970, Kerry stood aside so another candidate could get the Democratic nomination to run for a seat in the U.S. House of Representatives. His next attempt at seeking elected office came in 1972. He did have one problem. Because he had moved so much growing up, he did not have long-term roots in any specific part of Massachusetts. Kerry began 1972 as a resident of Waltham, Massachusetts, a suburb west of Boston. Democrat Robert F. Drinan, whom Kerry was not likely to challenge, represented this district. In early February, Kerry's wife, Julia, bought a house in Worcester, in another congressional district, where Kerry thought of challenging a conservative Democrat in the primary. But they never moved into the house.

In late March 1972, Kerry learned that Republican congressman F. Bradford Morse was going to be appointed under-secretary-general of the United Nations. Morse represented what was then the Fifth Congressional District, centered by the industrial city of Lowell, north of Boston.

Kerry and his wife rented an apartment in Lowell, and Kerry set out to run from that district. Kerry may not have fully realized what he was in for. "Politics has always been blood sport in blue-collar Lowell," is the way the *Boston Globe* series on Kerry described his choice of political base. Lowell, along with nearby Lawrence, had been the center of the Massachusetts textile industry from the start of the Industrial Revolution until the early 1940s, when most of the industry began to move to the cheaper labor market of the southern United States. Lowell was also hard hit by the national recession in the early 1970s, with an unemployment rate over ten percent. At the time Kerry thought of running, it was described as "an old mill city—a typical blue-collar, mostly Roman Catholic, New England city."

Lowell's population was made up of several ethnic groups, including Irish, French Canadian, Greek, Polish, Lithuanian, Portuguese, and Armenian. The textile industry had provided employment for many of these immigrants for generations, and area politics thrived on patronage and favors. It was also socially conservative and heavily Catholic. Working-class Democrats in Lowell were typical of the so-called "silent majority" that Richard Nixon counted on to support his policies. Lowell voters were likely to be turned off by antiwar protests.

Kerry was a Democrat and a Catholic, but was more liberal than the bulk of his potential constituents. More

Kerry's headquarters in Lowell, Massachusetts, out of which he ran his 1972 campaign for Congress. *(AP Photo)*

importantly, he was an outsider. Kerry himself has said, "I can understand people who were angry at me. I came into the district, crash, 'Here I am.' There was a brashness to it. . . . if I had known what I know today about politics, I'm not sure I would have done it."

Kerry had nine opponents in the Democratic primary. His eventual opponent, Paul Cronin, had three opponents in the Republican primary. A conservative Lowell Democrat, Roger P. Durkin, ran as an independent. Kerry ran a very expensive and sophisticated campaign, supported by many contributors from outside the district—a fact that would come back to haunt him in the general election campaign. His campaign also attended to constituent service—often key to political success as the individual voters helped are likely to tell friends and family—doing such things as distributing leaflets describing government services to the elderly and preparing a consumer guide comparing supermarket prices in the district.

The day before the primary election, Kerry's younger brother, Cameron, and an associate were arrested at two in the morning in the building housing campaign offices for Kerry and one of his opponents. They were near the area containing phones lines for the entire building. That day the afternoon *Lowell Sun's* headline read, "Kerry brother arrested in Lowell 'Watergate.'" This was not long after the June 1972 Watergate break-in, which would eventually bring down the Nixon administration.

The Kerry camp declared that the incident was a trap. Cameron and the other man had responded to an anonymous phone call claiming someone was out to damage the phone lines and cripple a last minute effort to get out the vote by calling people to remind them to go to the polls. Charges were dropped a year later.

Kerry won the primary with twenty-eight percent of the vote, an excellent showing in a ten-candidate field. He carried eighteen of the twenty-two smaller towns in the district. He averaged seventy-five percent of the vote in the outlying areas.

Kerry was favored in the general election campaign. One poll put him twenty-six points ahead of Republican Paul Cronin. However, Kerry faced opposition from Clement C. Costello, the activist and ultraconservative editor of the *Lowell Sun*. Costello held his ammunition and made his attacks on Kerry near the end of the campaign, which gave him little time to respond. When they came, the newspaper attacks were steady and harsh, focusing on Kerry's "district shopping," his accepting campaign contributions from outside the district, and his antiwar activism.

On October 29, 1972, Costello endorsed Paul Cronin. On October 30, he wrote an editorial entitled "Kerry the New Soldier." The editorial said that Kerry "put the good name that he had won for himself in Vietnam on the line in defense of the radical peace agitators. In fact, he led them . . . Mr. Kerry's national reputation as a radical leftist war protestor which he himself created in an immature judgment of America's role in the Vietnam will not inspire respect."

The final blow to Kerry's chances came a few days before the election when the independent Durkin withdrew and threw his support to Cronin, who won the election by nine percentage points. Three decades later the publisher of the *Lowell Sun* remarked that without his paper's attacks, Kerry would have been elected. Kerry has also blamed his defeat on the *Sun*, as well as his own failure to respond quickly to its charges.

After the defeat, Kerry was unemployed and faced with a large campaign debt. He had to find a way to earn a living. In September 1973, soon after the birth of his first child, daughter Alexandra, Kerry began law school at Boston College. He also worked part time as a radio talk-show host and spent a period as the executive director of a state financial watchdog group.

Richard Nixon was forced out of office in August 1974 because of his administration's attempts to obstruct justice and for lying about its participation in the June 1972 burglary of the Democratic National Committee headquarters. In the fall of 1974, Paul Cronin was defeated in his reelection bid by Paul Tsongas. Kerry, who had been considering running again in

Paul Tsongas. *(AP Photo)*

1974, decided instead to help Tsongas. He turned over his contributor and contact lists to Tsongas.

In the spring of 1976, Kerry, now thirty-two, graduated from law school and passed the bar exam. He then shocked many of his friends by joining the Middlesex County District Attorney's office. Middlesex County encompasses suburban Boston to the north, northwest, and west.

Ronald F. Rosenblith, a former Kerry aide and fund-raiser, recently said that "[m]ost people would have told you then that it was a Nixonian-Agnew thing to become a prosecutor and law-and-order. They couldn't understand why this great progressive shining voice that could articulate things so well on our side would do this." Kerry himself, when told he seemed more a natural fit in a public defender's office, responded, "That's a stereotype of the worst order and a total knee-jerk reaction."

Kerry went on to say that he "always had a prosecutor's mind and a prosecutor's bent." Kerry's father had spent some time as a prosecutor before going to work for the Navy Department, and told him it was a good way to get trial practice.

Kerry's second daughter, Vanessa, was born on New Year's Eve, 1976. A few weeks later, although he had only been in the office for eight months, Middlesex district attorney John J. Droney appointed Kerry first assistant district attorney. Droney was running for re-election in 1978. But he also had the serious muscular condition known as Lou Gehrig's disease. He moved slowly and could not speak very clearly.

While Kerry worked as first assistant district attorney, he arranged for federal funding to triple the staff, improve operations, and to launch white collar and organized crime units plus a victim's aid unit.

Some more senior attorneys in the district attorney's office resented Kerry's rapid promotion. Many of the newer staff members liked Kerry and appreciated what he was trying to accomplish. Thomas Hoopes, a prosecutor hired by Kerry, remembered, "To become first assistant, traditionally, you had to pay your dues and work your way up. Mr. Droney jumped John over virtually all of that, and, in the end, it makes no difference. John built this thing from a sleepy backwater operation into a real powerhouse."

Although not everyone liked Kerry, he did often show care and discretion. He once got a call from the chief of police of Somerville, who said his department was about to arrest the mayor of Somerville for the rape of another man. Kerry told the chief to come to his office first. After discussing the case for a while, Kerry decided to invite the alleged victim to take a lie-detector test. As soon as the man got to the office, he confessed that the accusation was lie. Kerry later said that had the accusation been made public, even if it was later proved false, the mayor's reputation would have been destroyed.

One sensational case Kerry handled personally was that of George Edgerly. In 1959, the body of Edgerly's wife had been fished out of the Merrimack River. Edgerly was charged with her death. Evidence had come to light that Edgerly was having sexual affairs with his wife's mother and sisters.

During the trial, Edgerly's attorney, John Tobin, allowed the jury to learn that Edgerly had failed a polygraph (lie-detector) examination. This was a mistake that Tobin had to correct. Only two men in the country knew enough about the then-new technology to question the polygraph examiner and, hopefully, discredit the evidence. One had just become a judge. The other was the little-known F. Lee Bailey, who would become one of the most famous attorneys in the country. Bailey's expert cross-examination destroyed the value of the polygraph evidence and won an acquittal.

On his release, Edgerly went to work at a Chevrolet dealership in Lowell. He soon became involved with a scheme to submit fake warranty claims to General Motors, Chevrolet's parent company. When General Motors sent a man named Francis Smith to investigate the operation in Lowell, Smith was murdered. Edgerly was charged with this murder. While the case was underway, he was convicted of fraud. Edgerly soon became a suspect in a rape case. The alleged victim was a prostitute who also claimed, falsely, that she had been offered $2,000 by Edgerly to drop the case.

One of Kerry's former colleagues remembered, "Kerry told me this Edgerly was a lucky guy. This could be a snakebit case. It was not a slam-dunk. Nobody was going to try that case if you were just looking to put a notch in your belt." Kerry decided to try the rape case himself. He later stated, "The victim was very suspect because of her lifestyle and background. The bottom line was that she did not consent, the bottom line was that she had been raped. . . . I thought she deserved justice like anyone else."

Kerry faced another problem. Rape shield laws were not yet in effect, so the victim's sexual history could be brought up. The witness testified to the rape itself, where both Edgerly and another man made the woman have sex in the back of a car. The witness testified that Edgerly had not offered her $2,000, but that she asked for the money and that Edgerly agreed to pay. Edgerly was convicted of rape. Kerry had overcome two serious problems with his main witness: she had lied to the police, and her profession made her claims less sympathetic to a jury. Edgerly was also later convicted of the murder of Francis Smith. He remains in prison.

Kerry's boss, John Droney, faced a serious primary challenge from L. Scott Harshbarger in 1978. Kerry served as the ill Droney's surrogate in the campaign, defending the work of the district attorney's office. Droney won a close primary victory. After the election, feeling invigorated, he began to retake control of his office. Kerry soon decided to leave the office and go into private practice. Harshbarger defeated Droney in the 1982 primary.

Kerry and Roanne Sragow, another former assistant district attorney, opened a law partnership. They both wanted a break from criminal law so they specialized in wrongful death, medical malpractice, and trade secrets. They even handled a series of cases involving the use of carpet fibers as hair transplants. Kerry recalled, "They represented a really grotesque abuse of people." They won their first case and settled the rest. Massachusetts authorities clamped down on such implants.

At the same time Kerry's career was going well, his wife's health was declining. Though it would be years before she was diagnosed, Julia suffered from clinical depression. In 1980, she was on the verge of suicide. She described her feelings in the introduction to a 1994 book:

> February 1980, five months after my 36th birthday, my mind ravaged by corroding voices, my body defeated by bone-rattling panics, I sat on the edge of my bed minutes from taking my life. For weeks I had silently prepared my death. I believed I was a failure. I could no longer pretend I was of use to my husband or children. I was too tired. I needed to lie down, curled up, never to wake again. I knew that, once I was gone, my family and friends would be relieved of the burden of my incompetency. . . . [It was] a nightmare life defined by self-hate and self-doubt, a life sapped by the pain of depression from which, I had come to believe, death was the only escape.

Julia's plan to take her own life was interrupted by a phone call. Though Kerry was sympathetic during this time, Julia concealed the depths of her feelings from him and their marriage suffered.

Kerry learned several things from these years of his life. The 1972 race for Congress taught him the advantages of timing and the need to retaliate when attacked politically. His years as a prosecutor honed his skill at persistently digging for facts, for the truth. He also developed his ability to learn from mistakes. He later admitted to several major mistakes in his 1972 campaign for Congress. He failed to lay the proper groundwork in a district to which he had just moved. He failed to respond to the *Lowell Sun.*

His legal practice, particularly as a district attorney, showed a growing ability to adapt to political reality, and to recognize the need to pay political "dues." His work also showed a commitment to use government for the public good.

In 1982, Kerry learned that Thomas P. O'Neill III, whose father was then speaker of the United States House of Representatives, was giving up the post of lieutenant governor to run for governor. Kerry set his sights on O'Neill's office.

Chapter Six

Lieutenant Governor

The office of lieutenant governor of Massachusetts is often a stepping-stone to higher office. Kerry was one of five candidates in the 1982 Democratic primary. The current lieutenant governor, Tommy O'Neill, had given up his post to challenge the incumbent, Edward J. King, for the governor's post. The third Democratic candidate in the gubernatorial primary was former governor Michael Dukakis, who had lost to King four years earlier.

Kerry had to first prepare for a Democratic endorsement convention in May. Winning the endorsement would be valuable, but not decisive, for winning the September primary. Kerry had to stand out among the five major candidates, two other men and two women. As the *Boston Globe* reported in a 2003 series on Kerry, "As he began his comeback in early 1982, John F. Kerry found a political landscape as changed as he was by events of the previous ten years. Gone was the rock star aura of the 1972 congressional candidate. . . . In the button-down Reagan era, Kerry was now Mr. Mainstream."

In the race for governor, Michael Dukakis was running a tough, anti-corruption campaign against King, whose administration had major corruption problems, including the conviction of a cabinet secretary on corruption charges and the suicide of a senior civil servant in the tax department.

Kerry came prepared to the convention. He ran as a progressive with a law-and-order background as a prosecutor. He was a proponent of public investment in infrastructure, such as highways and public transportation. He also championed a nuclear weapons freeze: the idea that all countries, but primarily the United States and the Soviet Union, should agree not to increase their nuclear weapon stockpile. This was a curious stand to take for someone running for an office that had little real influence over state policy, let alone national defense policy.

Kerry was not a favorite of the party leadership, so he won only fifteen percent of the delegate votes at the convention and barely qualified for the September ballot. However, his floor managers worked to insure that Lois Pines, a former state legislator, also got enough votes to get on the ballot. The convention's winner was Evelyn Murphy for a total of two women on the ballot.

Kerry won the September primary with twenty-nine percent of the vote. Murphy was 40,000 votes behind out of 1.1 million cast. Interestingly, Kerry carried Lowell, which had rejected him in 1972. The November election proved to be no challenge. Both Dukakis and Kerry won handily.

Massachusetts governor Michael Dukakis with Lieutenant Governor John Kerry in 1982. *(Library of Congress)*

During the 1982 campaign Kerry's marriage finally collapsed. It had suffered from the pressure of his career and Julia's struggle with depression. "I tried to be happy for him," she later wrote, "but after fourteen years as a political wife I associated politics with anger, fear, and loneliness." Even after they separated in June of 1982, Julia continued to make campaign appearances with her husband.

Kerry tried to concentrate on his campaign. He later admitted, "When I get focused and set out to do something, I'm pretty good at staying focused."

Kerry had few official duties as lieutenant governor. Basically he was acting governor if the governor left the state, and chaired meetings of the Executive Council, whose primary function was to confirm or reject judicial nominees. But Dukakis gave Kerry things to do. He considered Kerry a loyal team player. Kerry coordinated federal relations. He was also vice chairman of the Anti-Crime Council, of which Dukakis was chairman, and helped to craft a computer crimes bill.

In addition to the work given him by Governor Dukakis, Kerry made it a point to maintain a relationship with his daughters, who were living with their mother. He had learned a lesson from his father. Keeping his family together was difficult at times, and activities with his daughters had to be scheduled in with his work as lieutenant governor.

Kerry also became a national figure in the effort to fight acid rain. Industrial pollution was increasing the corrosiveness of rain and the damage it caused to the environment. Acid rain was mostly produced in the industrial Midwest, but because of wind currents, most of the damage was done in the Northeast. At the February 1984 meeting of the National Governors Association, Kerry managed to get a resolution passed calling for cuts in sulfur dioxide emissions.

On January 12, 1984, just over a year after taking office, Kerry was in the Black Forest of Germany on an acid rain fact-finding trip. He was awakened early in the morning and told that the next day, in Boston, his old comrade Paul Tsongas, who was now a U.S. senator, was going to announce that he would be retiring from office because of his struggle with the cancer that would eventually kill him.

This was an opportunity for Kerry. "But it was tricky,"

Kerry later remembered. He had just been elected lieutenant governor and he knew better than most how much the charge of excessive ambition could hurt a politician. He finally decided to take the risk. He later explained that "it was the right place for me in terms of the things that were my passions. The issue of war and peace was on the table again." Two weeks after Paul Tsongas announced his retirement, Kerry entered the race.

The four-man race for the Democratic nomination quickly became a two-man race between Kerry and Representative James Shannon. Kerry and Shannon held similar views. The nuclear freeze became an issue during this campaign when a pro-freeze organization sent questionnaires to all Senate candidates. Shannon received a one hundred percent score on the questionnaire, Kerry only a ninety-four.

Shannon was a tough opponent. Kerry, however, was very good under pressure—sometimes better under pressure than when things were going well. His former brother-in-law, David Thorne, who has remained Kerry's closest friend, told an interviewer, "When [Kerry] is in a fight, he rises to the moment like nobody else I've seen. He has a great instinct for figuring out, under pressure, what is necessary for survival. The downside is, when he's not under pressure he can sometimes wander around."

Kerry took advantage of a Shannon campaign error. Shannon did not serve in the military but he found some Vietnam veterans willing to attack Kerry for his antiwar work. During the next to last debate, Shannon challenged Kerry's antiwar stance by saying, "If you

Kerry with his daughters Alexandra and Vanessa on the night of his 1984 Senate win.
(George Butler / Contact Press Images)

felt that strongly about the war, you would not have gone." The next day, Kerry's headquarters received calls from veterans, many of whom had been drafted, infuriated by Shannon's statement. They had not asked to go to war.

Two days later, in the next televised debate, Kerry responded by telling Shannon, "You impugn the service of veterans in that war by saying they are somehow dopes or wrong for going." Shannon refused to apologize, which further alienated many of the Vietnam veterans among Democratic voters. Kerry beat Shannon and won the Democratic nomination.

In the November election, Republican president Reagan won Massachusetts in his bid for reelection, but the Democratic Kerry easily won election to the Senate.

Chapter Seven

The Senate

John Kerry has never been happy with the coverage he has received from the *Boston Globe*, the major local newspaper in the Boston area. In 2004, when the editors of the *Globe* adapted and enlarged to book length an earlier biographical series on Kerry, they began it with a ten-page preface explaining their side of the dispute.

Michael Janeway, editor of the *Globe* in 1984, put his finger on an image problem Kerry brought to the Senate. Kerry invited Janeway to breakfast after the 1984 election. As Janeway recalled, "He wanted to know why we were so rough on him. I reminded him about [former Speaker of the United States House of Representatives] Sam Rayburn's classic political categories. I said 'John, there are workhorses and show horses, and I guess our staff considers you a show horse.'"

When Kerry was asked about his reputation for political opportunism, he said, "I think I got something of a rap ten years ago which I brought on myself, partly because of my impatience and partly through my total focus, my absolute, total commitment to ending the war. I think there was an element of brashness. . . . I admit that now . . . Why do people dwell on that so?"

Kerry had a more immediate situation to work out when he arrived in the Senate in 1985. He had to figure out how to get along with and how to work with the senior senator from Massachusetts, Edward Kennedy, who had been in the Senate for twenty-two years when Kerry arrived.

Kerry had two committee choices on his arrival in Washington. One was to join the Senate Appropriations Committee. Members of this committee spend money,

Massachusetts senior senator Edward Kennedy in 1985. *(AP Photo)*

frequently in their own districts. This means jobs for voters and profits for local business leaders and is an excellent way to keep one's job in the Senate. This was not Kerry's style. Not long after arriving, Kerry told an interviewer, "I came to do a job, not join a club."

Kerry chose the Senate Foreign Affairs Committee as his primary assignment. The Foreign Affairs Committee had lost some of the glamour it had when Kerry testified before it fourteen years earlier. To Kerry the committee was "about war and peace. We were entering an illegal war in Latin America. One of the lessons of Vietnam was about lying, about people who hide the truth from the American people, and there was a real parallel in Latin America." The "illegal war" Kerry referred to was in Nicaragua.

A few months into his first term, an aide to Massachusetts governor Michael Dukakis visited Kerry in Washington. The aide had known how interested and involved Kerry had been in domestic issues while lieutenant governor and asked why Kerry was not trying to shape policy by mastering a domestic issue. Kerry responded, "That just isn't me. I've always been more drawn to the investigative power—to figure out what's wrong and go after it."

Kerry had always been good at investigations. A recent analysis of his career determined that Kerry's investigations "have been unusually thorough by congressional standards." He applied the lessons of his legal career, particularly his work as a prosecutor who had to dig for facts and use these facts to determine the truth, to the Senate. He always had some idea of where to look for information and how to evaluate what he found. He also had the determination to keep looking.

One former aide and investigator, Jack Blum, credits Kerry's investigatory drive to what Blum calls the "Vietnam veteran syndrome. You come home and discover that the people who are running the war are just interested in covering their ass; meanwhile, real people are dying."

Kerry was sent to the Senate in the same election year President Ronald Reagan was reelected by a landslide. Reagan and his administration saw his reelection as support for more active confrontation of the Soviet Union and its allies and supporters throughout the world.

In April 1985, just three months after he took office, Kerry and fellow freshman senator Tom Harkin of Iowa flew to Managua, the capitol of Nicaragua, for a fact-finding mission. In 1979, a leftist group known as the Sandinistas had overthrown the American-supported dictator of Nicaragua. When the Reagan administration came to power, they began secretly funding and training a group of anti-Sandinista rebels known as the "contras." After learning that the CIA had mined Nicaraguan harbors, and in reaction to the Contras' reputation for murdering civilians, Congress ordered the aid cut off.

Kerry and Harkin recognized that the Sandinista government was repressive. They made it clear they were not backing the Sandinistas but were opposed to the United States getting involved in a civil war. Kerry and Harkin brought back an offer from the Sandinista government to make peace with the Contras. The written offer included a declaration that the Sandinistas would improve civil liberties.

The offer was rejected by the Reagan administration. They wanted to overthrow the Sandinista government. Reagan and his people were at the height of their desire to confront the Soviet Union and its allies throughout the world. Kerry was accused of being soft on a Communist government. He responded, "The Sandinistas' failings should not be an excuse for ignoring opportunities for peace."

The day after Kerry returned to Washington, Daniel Ortega, the leader of the Sandinista government, flew to Moscow, the capital of the Soviet Union, where he was granted a $200 million loan. This outraged many in Congress, including several Democrats, who voted to approve nonmilitary aid to the Contras.

U.S. support of the Contras was one of the most controversial issues of the 1980s. It soon became even more controversial when it was revealed that the Reagan administration had been defying Congress, and breaking the law, in order to supply the anti-Communist rebels. What shocked many Americans was how they went about raising the funds to send to Nicaragua.

The scheme concocted by President Reagan's national security advisor and others to circumvent the Congressional ban on funding the Contras was to raise the money by selling weapons to the Iranian government—the sworn enemy of the United States.

In 1985, the Reagan administration's desire to fund the Contras became ensnared in the effort to free seven American hostages held in Lebanon by the radical Shiite Muslim group Hezbollah. Reagan and some of his advisors, against his own stated policy of refusing to negotiate with terrorists and against American calls for our allies to present a united front, decided to negotiate indirectly with the terrorists. The Reagan administration agreed to sell arms to Iran, which was in the middle of a terrible war with Saddam Hussein's Iraq, in order to gain Iranian support for freeing the hostages. The money that was made from the sales of the weapons was secretly sent to the Contras.

Late in 1985, Kerry's office began to get tips about what was going on with the weapons and money transfers. Kerry worried about a repeat of Vietnam. Here was another White House lying to the public about a military operation. Kerry told his staff to look into what was going on. According to his counsel, Jonathan Winer, "It was like a detective story at that point. [Clues pointed to] violations of U.S. law by the Reagan administration."

The behind-the-scenes operational manager of the scheme funding the Contras was an obscure colonel in the Pentagon: Oliver North. North began to get nervous about what Kerry might uncover. Republican staff members from the Foreign Affairs Committee were leaking information on Kerry's probe to the Reagan administration. In an attempt to stop Kerry's investigation, North accused Kerry's main witness, Jack Terrell, of being a

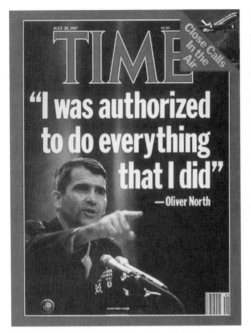

Oliver North on the cover of *Time* during the Iran-Contra investigation.

spy and potential presidential assassin. The FBI began to follow Terrell and soon pressured him into taking a lie detector test. Terrell was determined to be no threat to the president. However, the intimidation worked and he did not testify.

In 1986, Reagan authorized the Central Intelligence Agency to sell arms directly to Iran. Oliver North coordinated this activity. When foreign funds for the Contras dried up, North inflated the price Iranians were charged and diverted the excess funds to Swiss bank accounts. This money was used to fund the Contras.

In the summer of 1986, Kerry persuaded the Foreign Affairs Committee to start a formal investigation of the Contras, focusing in particular on the charges that they were smuggling drugs into the United States to help fund their operations. Some Republican senators on the committee were being pressured by North to back the administration. Kerry, however, had an ace in the hole. He had already discussed the issue with Jesse Helms, senior Republican member of the committee and one of the most conservative members of the Senate. Helms was a strong Contra supporter, but he told another senator on the committee, "I will tell you what I do not support, and John Kerry and I have talked about this: anybody sending drugs into this country. I do not care whose side they are on." Helms's support for the investigation was the turning point: the committee decided to investigate the possible Contra-drug connection.

While this investigation was underway, on October 5, 1986, a plane was shot down in Nicaragua. Documents in the wreckage connected the plane to the CIA. A surviving crew member said he was involved in CIA efforts to arm the Contras. About a month later, a newspaper in Lebanon broke the whole story, including the sale of arms to Iran.

Kerry was the senator most responsible for launching the investigation into the Iran-Contra scandal, but when a special investigating committee was formed in early 1987, he was left off. If he had been appointed, it would have made it easier for the Reagan administration to claim the investigation was simply a political witchhunt. According to a senior aide, "He was told early on that they were not going to put him on it. He was too junior and too controversial." Kerry was given instead the chairmanship of the Subcommittee on Terrorism, Narcotics, and International Operations, with a charter to look into the Contra-drug connection.

In a report issued in 1989, Kerry's subcommittee found evidence that the CIA and other American agencies had turned a blind eye to drug trafficking on the fringes of the Contra network. Later investigations by inspectors general at the CIA and Justice Department confirmed these conclusions. Kerry found no evidence that the CIA and or any other government agency had run or sanctioned a Contra drug ring.

A spin-off of the Contra-drug investigation examined reports that Panamanian dictator Manuel Noriega was involved in drug trafficking. Kerry's probe found that Noriega was shipping money out of Panama with the help of a bank called the Bank of Credit and Commerce International, better known as BCCI. BCCI was very popular with clients such as arms dealers and drug dealers. BCCI employees asked few questions about where the money came from. The CIA even used the bank when it needed to hide money for its own activities. Kerry's 1988 investigation helped to close the bank three years later.

In 1988, Kerry took on a major task for the Democratic Party in the Senate. He was selected as chair of the Democratic Senatorial Campaign Committee. His job was to raise money to elect and reelect Democratic senators. The Republicans have a similar organization. During his 1984 campaign, Kerry had refused to accept money from political action committees, better known as PACs. He now intended to go after such money for his colleagues. Kerry did such a good job that in the 1990 elections, when the best the Democrats could hope for was to keep the seats they had, they picked up one seat. Kerry was easily reelected in 1990.

Kerry's personal life was unsettled during this period. His divorce from Julia became final in 1988. Julia
had provided most of the family's money and he was
now strapped for cash. A senator made approximately
$150,000 per year at this time, but the expense of main-
taining two residences—in the Washington, D.C., area
and at home—and frequent trips back and forth to stay
in contact with the voters added up. He was also paying
child support and tuition. Kerry flew back to Boston
most weekends. There were periods when, having no
residence himself, he had to stay with friends when
back in Massachusetts.

Federal prosecutor William F. Weld had decided to
run for governor of Massachusetts in 1990, though he
had thought about running for the Senate. Weld was
elected governor. Six years later, he and Kerry would
meet in one of the most exciting races of the decade.

Chapter Eight

Close Call

The first issue John Kerry faced on his return to the Senate in 1991 was the Iraqi invasion of Kuwait that began on August 2, 1990. Saddam Hussein, the dictator of Iraq, declared Kuwait to be the nineteenth province of Iraq. The invasion surprised the world because it had only been two years since the inconclusive settlement of Iraq's bloody eight-year war with Iran. Most observers thought Iraq was much too weak to attempt such a bold move.

The question was how the United States and the rest of the world would react to Hussein's actions. Hussein had shown a brutal ruthlessness in using any weapons at his disposal. He employed poison gas against Iran as well as against dissident Kurds in the north of Iraq.

Urged on by visiting British prime minister Margaret Thatcher, President George H. W. Bush declared that the takeover of Kuwait was unacceptable. Bush then began a two-pronged effort to get Hussein out of Ku-

The Persian Gulf region in 1991. Saddam Hussein's military had invaded the tiny oil-rich country of Kuwait on August 2, 1990.

wait. He tried peaceful measures, including strong United Nations sanctions. He also convinced the United Nations Security Council to authorize the use of force if the Iraqis did not pull out of Kuwait by January 15, 1991. Bush asked Congress to approve a military strike if Hussein refused to withdraw. American troops were already being dispatched to Saudi Arabia. Bush was also arranging a multinational coalition, including forces from Britain, France, and several Arab countries.

The Iraqis were thought to have a powerful army. Their military was, at least numerically, the fourth largest in the world. The Iraqis also possessed chemical weapons and possibly biological weapons. They seemed like a formidable opponent, particularly if one did not look too carefully at the fact that in eight years, even while using chemical weapons, they had failed to defeat a weaker Iranian military.

Kerry thought the vote to support or to not support going to war with Iraq would be "the most important vote" of his Senate career. During most of his first term he had been concerned that Nicaragua would become another Vietnam-style quagmire. Kerry had helped to solve the problem before American troops were dispatched. Diplomacy and openness seemed to have settled the Nicaraguan issue. Perhaps similar diplomacy could work in Kuwait.

Kerry thought Hussein should be given more diplomatic "wiggle room" for maneuvering. "My greatest fear is this issue is too much box and not enough capacity to move out," Kerry said at the time. "That line is pointing in a very dangerous direction." He thought the White House should use quiet diplomatic channels to signal to Hussein a willingness to see Iraq's claims on specific Kuwaiti territory adjudicated in an international forum, if Hussein agreed to leave Kuwait.

On January 11, 1991, the Senate began to debate giving the president the authority to invade Iraq and free Kuwait. Democratic senator Sam Nunn of Georgia, chairman of the Senate Armed Services Committee, supported a powerful military, but he thought economic sanctions against Iraq should be given more time to work. Kerry agreed and spoke before the Senate in favor of continuing sanctions. He focused on avoiding the tragedy of another Vietnam, reminding his colleagues, "we are talking about war, about countless of our families torn apart by duty and commitment to our country, of countless lives put on hold." Kerry made it clear that he would support the use of force in appropriate circumstances, but that he did not consider this to be such a time.

On January 12, 1991, Congress voted to give President Bush the authority to use military action against Iraq. Kerry was one of forty-seven senators who opposed authorizing force. The first American war with Iraq, Operation Desert Storm, began the evening of January 16, 1991, Washington, D.C., time. Attack helicopters cut a hole in the coverage area of Iraqi radar nets, and American attacks destroyed the Iraqi command structure. Six weeks later, when the ground campaign finally began, it took just one hundred hours to drive Hussein's forces out of Kuwait.

Kerry's next foreign policy issue arose during a spring 1991 trip to the Middle East. Kerry found himself seated across from Senator John McCain, the Republican from Arizona, in a cramped and noisy military transport plane.

McCain was also a Vietnam veteran who had been held prisoner in North Vietnam for more than five years. McCain had been distrustful of Kerry at first. He thought Kerry too much of a hot shot and disagreed with his antiwar activism after returning from Vietnam.

Kerry and McCain now had a chance to talk about

their experiences in Vietnam. Kerry said, "I asked a lot of questions about him, and he of me, and we talked about how he felt about his war, and my war." Both men began to realize the time had come to put the war to rest. The military had supposedly gotten over the "Vietnam syndrome" with the Desert Storm victory over Iraq. But many others in the U.S. were still preoccupied with the unresolved issues resulting from the war.

The first issue to settle as far as the American public was concerned was the issue of the missing in action soldiers, or MIA. Every war produces thousands of such cases in which soldiers just disappear. More than 2,000 Americans were still MIA from the Vietnam War. Most were assumed to be dead. Jungle warfare, of the sort that often occurred in Vietnam, increased the likelihood that soldiers could be killed and their bodies never found.

Senators John Kerry and John McCain confer during a hearing of the Senate Select Committee on POW/MIA Affairs on December 1, 1992. *(AP Photo)*

However, a small but active "MIA lobby" insisted their loved ones could still be alive in Southeast Asia. Some politicians latched on to this issue as a way to improve their political fortunes. In 1991, Kerry was made chairman of the newly formed Senate Select Committee on POW-MIA Affairs (POW stands for Prisoner of War—some believed Vietnam still held American captives). The committee would stay in existence for one year, unless its charter was renewed. Kerry wanted McCain to serve as vice chairman. McCain, however, was even less popular with the POW-MIA activists than Kerry because he rejected their theories.

Every member of his staff had urged Kerry not to take the job. He would be risking the political wrath of the families of the missing. Kerry was willing to take the risk to provide an objective examination of the issue. He explained, "I thought that as a Vietnam veteran that I have an obligation to my fellow Vietnam veterans to get the answers."

Senator Robert Smith of New Hampshire became the Republican co-chairman. Kerry left for Vietnam in August 1991, his first trip there since 1969, to discuss the issue with the Vietnamese government. Kerry brought an incentive with him—the possibility of renewed trade and diplomatic relations with the United States. On a second trip, in November 1992, Kerry brought a letter from President Bush specifically promising improved relations in return for increased cooperation on the POW-MIA issue. Kerry and his committee received this cooperation from the Vietnamese.

John Kerry

John McCain later commented on the expertise Kerry showed at handling people at committee hearings: "He has a capacity for patience. . . . It's a vital ingredient for getting results. I acquired profound appreciation for his excellent work on a terribly difficult, emotional issue."

A few months later, Kerry and his committee reported, unanimously, that there was no way to prove that any Americans remained alive in Vietnam. Kerry also said there was no indication of any efforts to hide American prisoners.

In 1994, the Republicans took over control of both the Senate and the House of Representatives. Kerry blamed the Democratic defeat on blunders by the Clinton administration, which had come to power in 1993. He even claimed to be "delighted by the shakeup. . . . I have to be honest in acknowledging that mistakes were made and that the agenda was not as focused as it should have been. To not acknowledge that is to court further disaster." These might have been honest comments, but they angered the Democratic establishment in Massachusetts.

Kerry's personal life also changed in these years. By 1995 he had been separated from his first wife for thirteen years, formally divorced for seven. On May 26, 1995, he married Teresa Heinz, the widow of Senator John Heinz of Pennsylvania. Senator Heinz had been killed in a plane crash in 1991. Teresa had grown up in Mozambique. Her father was Portuguese and her mother of mixed European ancestry. She speaks several languages fluently and has a slight Portuguese accent. Teresa had studied literature in South Africa, where she demonstrated against racial apartheid. In Pittsburgh, the Heinz family home, she developed a reputation for generosity to charitable causes, for speaking her mind, and for having a volatile temper. She is also the heir to the Heinz ketchup fortune.

Kerry and Teresa had known each other casually while Senator Heinz was still alive. They renewed their acquaintance in 1992 at an environ-

Teresa Heinz Kerry. *(AP Photo)*

mental conference in Brazil, began dating in early 1994, and became engaged later that year. Heinz, who is five years older than Kerry, provided him with the personal stability he had been lacking since his marriage to Julia Thorne had started to decline.

On July 11, 1995, President Bill Clinton announced the restoration of diplomatic relations between the United States and Vietnam. John Kerry and John McCain, Vietnam combat veterans, stood with President Clinton when he made this announcement.

Kerry ran for a third term in the Senate in 1996. Kerry's Republican challenger was Governor William Weld, who had been reelected in 1994 with seventy-one percent of the vote. Weld has much in common with Kerry. He is from a similar background, has a good education, and is a highly skilled politician. He is also very ambitious. Weld was thinking of running for president in 2000 if he won the 1996 Senate race. Kerry was also thinking about running in 2000.

Weld and Kerry debated seven times during the 1996 campaign, which became the most closely watched Senate race in the country. The campaign focused on domestic topics. In one debate, Kerry flubbed a response to the question of naming three things he had done for the people of Massachusetts. But Kerry was still an

Governor William Weld and Senator John Kerry shake hands after their debate during the 1996 Senate race. *(AP Photo)*

excellent debater and was not likely to repeat such a major mistake. Weld has said that "[i]n terms of effectiveness as a debater, [Kerry] is as good as it gets."

At one of the debates, a question from Weld on the death penalty for a cop killer allowed Kerry to start a response by saying, "I know something about killing." He then went on to say that he did not think the state honored life by sanctioning killing. Aside from deflecting a potentially damaging question, Kerry also managed to remind voters of his war record. Weld had been deferred from military service due to a bad back. On other occasions Kerry managed to remind the voters of Weld's connection with the party of Newt Gingrich, Republican Speaker of the House of Representatives, who was not popular in Massachusetts.

In the end, Kerry managed to hold off Weld's challenge and secured a third term in the U.S. Senate. Once the election was over, Kerry began to make a concentrated effort to mend fences with Massachusetts Democratic leaders and to concentrate on serving and protecting his political base. Even in Lowell, the center of Kerry's unsuccessful 1972 campaign, the mayor commented, "A lot of people thought he was aloof. But his staff was always there for us. He didn't let Lowell's needs go by the wayside." Kerry would be easily re-elected the next time he ran, in 2002.

Chapter Nine

Political Culmination

President Bill Clinton, who had first been elected in 1992, was not allowed to run for reelection in 2000. Kerry considered running for the Democratic nomination to succeed him. In the end, he decided that Vice President Al Gore's lead was insurmountable.

The presidential election of 2000, between Democratic Vice President Albert Gore and Republican George W. Bush of Texas, was the closest in U.S. history. Gore won a half million more votes than Bush but, due to the way Gore's support was distributed across the nation, Bush won the election in the Electoral College. But even there the outcome was close and controversial. The vote in Florida turned out to be decisive. There was evidence of several voting irregularities in heavily Democratic areas of the state. In the end the election was decided by a 5-4 vote of the United States Supreme Court. This is the only time a presidential election has been decided by the Supreme Court.

After the 2000 election, the U.S. Senate was split fifty-fifty. Under the Constitution, the vice president decided tie votes, which left the Republicans in charge when the Bush administration took office. Then, in April 2001, Senator Jim Jeffords of Vermont announced that he had left the Republican Party and would become an independent, and that he would "caucus" with the Democrats. This gave Kerry's party control of the Senate and the power to choose committee leaders.

Five months later, on September 11, 2001, Kerry stopped by his office before heading to a 9:00 AM meeting of the Senate Democratic leadership. An aide told him that a plane had crashed into the North Tower of the World Trade Center in New York City. Rushing to a television, Kerry, a pilot, said, "This is no accident." He told the aide there was no way a pilot could accidentally hit the North Tower in clear weather.

At 9:03, while Kerry was in the leadership meeting, the entire country learned that Kerry was right when a second commercial airliner flew into the South Tower of the World Trade Center. Forty minutes later the Senators heard a loud boom in the distance as a third hijacked airliner crashed into the Pentagon, in Arlington, Virginia.

Seventeen minutes later, the South Tower in Manhattan crumbled. The phone rang in the Capitol room where the Senators were meeting. The White House was being evacuated. A fourth hijacked airliner was still in the air and presumed to be headed to Washington. Likely targets were the White House or the Capitol. (The commission investigating the September 11 attacks later re-

Smoke pours out of the World Trade Center shortly before the towers collapsed on the morning of September 11, 2001. The terrorist attacks on New York and Washington, D.C., would drastically change the political landscape during President Bush's first term. *(AP Photo)*

leased information indicating that the probable target was the Capitol Building.)

That evening, Kerry went on the CNN's talk show *Larry King Live.* He said that the United States must respond "boldly and bravely—not recklessly—but boldly. We must be prepared, absolutely, to move unilaterally, if we need to, to protect the honor and civility that we stand for. And I think everybody in this country would support that based on the proper response with the proper information." Three days later, Kerry joined in a unanimous Senate vote to give Bush broad powers to use force against those involved in the attacks.

When it became clear that the Taliban government in Afghanistan had sheltered members of Al Qaeda, the terrorist organization that carried out the attacks, Kerry supported the use of force. He even took a slightly harder line than Bush and said he thought American ground troops would be necessary to strike the Taliban. When the ground and air attacks were carried out in Afghanistan, the Taliban quickly fell and Al Qaeda was damaged, but their leadership, including Osama bin Laden, was not captured.

Kerry supported specific Bush administration actions against terrorism, but worried that the United States was not doing enough to address the basic causes of terrorism. Kerry said that the Americans were not doing enough to "face those questions about poverty and opportunity and governance and development" that he argued gave rise to terrorism. However, he rejected the argument that the United States brought the September 11 attacks on itself because of its policies in the Middle East.

A few weeks later, Kerry voted for the U.S. Patriot Act, which gave broad new powers to domestic law enforcement in order to combat terrorism. Kerry sponsored an amendment to the act allowing for increased government monitoring of money laundering (efforts to hide the origins of illegal funds) as a possible source of terrorist funding. Kerry also supported an act establishing the death penalty for terrorism-related murder of American citizens abroad. In the fall of 2002, Kerry voted to establish the Department of Homeland Security, gathering in one department all terrorism-related agencies except the CIA and the FBI.

Supporting the war on terrorism was a simple decision for Kerry. Though its specific actions might be debatable, the government was acting in response to a specific act against the United States: the attacks of September 11, 2001, which killed more than 2,700 people. When the Bush administration started to shift its focus to Iraq, the question of how best to fight terrorism became more problematic.

Saddam Hussein had been left in power in Iraq at the end of Operation Desert Storm and was still in power on September 11, 2001. Almost immediately, the Bush administration began publicly suggesting that there was a link between the hijackers and Hussein, though there was no strong evidence to support such a connection. Most intelligence pointed out that the very religious Osama bin Laden did not trust the secular Hussein, who in turn did not trust bin Laden.

Regardless of what most of the intelligence stated, President Bush's State of the Union speech to Congress in January 2002 made it clear that he was determined to make overthrowing Saddam Hussein part of the "war on terror." In this speech Bush labeled Hussein part of an "axis of evil," along with Iran and North Korea. Administration officials expressed the concern that Hussein was hiding stockpiles of "weapons of mass destruction," a term which soon found its way into general use. Weapons of mass destruction, or WMDs, are nuclear bombs and chemical and biological weapons.

Iraq had already used chemical weapons in the war against Iran in the early 1980s and against the Kurds in

1988. It had also at-
tempted to build a
nuclear reactor in
1981, but that project
had been destroyed
by an Israeli air strike.
Hussein had not used
any WMDs during
Desert Storm, and
since then there had
been a series of
United Nations-
sponsored inspec-
tions. Hussein had
thrown the inspec-

This image of Saddam Hussein in 2003 was taken from an Iraqi TV broadcast.

tors out in 1998 and refused to let them back into Iraq.
This convinced the Bush administration that he was
hiding weapons. They were also motivated to overthrow
Hussein in hopes of being able to establish a democratic government in Iraq that might influence the rest
of the turbulent region.

By October 2002, the Bush administration made it
clear that it was determined to invade and that it would
soon be asking Congress to authorize the use of force.
Hussein had allowed the weapons inspectors to return
to Iraq in 2002, and they had found no weapons, but the
Bush administration insisted he was not cooperating
fully enough.

When the vote came up to authorize a U.S. invasion
of Iraq, Kerry voted yes, with the understanding that

the United States would take the case to the United Nations Security Council before launching the attack. The Security Council agreed to renew inspections but refused to authorize the use of force.

On March 7, 2003, the head of the United Nations nuclear agency told the Security Council that his team in Iraq had found "no evidence of resumed nuclear activities." The other head of inspections in Iraq, Hans Blix, found no evidence of chemical or biological weapons. But he complained that the Iraqi government was not supplying evidence that these prohibited weapons had been destroyed.

Regardless of the lack of support from the United Nations, the Bush administration decided to go to war. On March 20, the United States staged a cruise missile attack, soon followed by an invasion of ground troops. After a short but bloody confrontation, Hussein was out of power and in hiding. Ultimately, winning the fight against the Iraqi military turned out to be the easy part. As soon as the official fighting was over, a rebellion made up of various groups angered by the U.S. invasion began. It continued even after formal control of the country was turned over to a transitional Iraqi government on July 1, 2004. No weapons of mass destruction were ever found and the search for them was officially ended in January 2005.

Kerry had already decided to run for president in 2004. He filed the necessary papers with the Federal Election Commission on December 4, 2002. On February 12, 2003, Kerry had surgery on his cancerous prostrate gland at Johns Hopkins Hospital in Baltimore. Doctors said the surgery was highly successful, but it took Kerry several weeks to recover and get back on the campaign trail. By the time he was back, the war in Iraq had started.

Kerry was considered the front-runner for the Democratic nomination until the fall of 2003 when Howard Dean, former governor of Vermont, surged to the front buoyed by a strong web-based fund-raising campaign. Dean was a more exciting candidate than the normally reserved Kerry. But, characteristically, Kerry did not collapse under the pressure. He reorganized his campaign in the fall.

Then Howard Dean began to make political mistakes. The first came right before Christmas in 2003 when Saddam Hussein, missing since the end of major combat in Iraq, was captured. When Hussein's capture was announced, Dean declared, "The capture of Saddam Hussein has not made America safer." Dean appeared to be saying that an apparent success in the war did not matter.

The first big challenge of the campaign, the Iowa caucus, took place on January 19, 2004. Kerry surprised many observers by coming from behind to take first place. North Carolina senator John Edwards was second, and former front-runner Howard Dean finished a distant third.

Kerry's effort in Iowa had been helped by the sudden appearance of Jim Rasmussen, the man he had pulled from the Mekong River while under attack in

Vietnam. Rasmussen was a registered Republican, but he said that he wanted to come to Iowa and tell the world how much he admired the man who had saved his life. His appearance with Kerry at a campaign rally received wide exposure in the press and began to shift votes in Kerry's favor.

A week later, Kerry easily won the New Hampshire primary. Then on March 2, 2004, Kerry won nine of ten primaries and secured the Democratic nomination.

After winning the nomination Kerry's next challenge was to pick a vice-presidential running mate. He considered several choices. In the end, he chose his most formidable challenger for the Democratic nomination, North Carolina senator John Edwards. Edwards had impressed many voters with his refusal to engage in negative politics and his ability to communicate with voters. The fact that he was from North Carolina and was the son of a textile worker would hopefully offset the image of Kerry as the privileged child of an upper-class Boston family.

John Forbes Kerry accepted the nomination of the Democratic Party for president of the United States on the night of July 29, 2004. In keeping with the modern American political practice, his speech was televised—though, that year, the three main television networks declined to cover most of the Democratic and Republican conventions.

Former senator Max Cleland of Georgia, who had lost an arm and both his legs in the Vietnam War, introduced Kerry. Cleland was also a dramatic choice because, although he was a decorated war hero, he had been defeated in his 2002 campaign in large part because of Republican ads that compared him to Osama bin Laden. Kerry made his way from the back of the Boston Civic Center through the crowded audience to the podium, shaking hands along the way.

Kerry began his speech by saluting the audience and saying, "I'm John Kerry, and I'm reporting for duty." Nomination acceptance speeches are the first opportunity for presidential candidates to introduce themselves to a national audience. The only other similar media events during the campaigns are debates.

Kerry's acceptance speech presented his themes and ideas for the upcoming campaign. In the beginning, Kerry said that his father "taught me that we are here for something bigger than ourselves," and "my parents inspired me to serve." This is the personal theme Kerry presented in the speech, the theme of a career dedicated to public service, to fulfilling a duty to give public service, to persistence in pursuit of appropriate goals. Kerry promised to guide the nation in a less confrontational foreign policy than he said the Bush administration had pursued. On domestic issues, he stated his intention of turning back what he said were George Bush's efforts to shift the tax burden from the wealthiest in society to the middle class. He pledged to spend more on education and to work harder to protect the country from domestic attack. But his main point was that President Bush had diverted attention away from the terrorists who had actually attacked the United

States in order to pursue a war against Iraq. He promised to not make this kind of mistake if he was elected president.

In most presidential campaigns there is a quiet period between the first and second convention. But in 2004, the days between the Democratic and Republican conventions were filled with an orchestrated attack against what many saw as Kerry's strongest point—his service in Vietnam. Kerry had long been aware that his anti-Vietnam War stance had enraged some veterans. There had been attacks against him for protesting the war ever since the ones orchestrated by the Nixon White House in 1971. Now many of these same veterans came together again. But this time they were well financed by wealthy contributors to the Republican Party. The veterans organized themselves into a group that called themselves Swift Boat Veterans for Truth and, led by Kerry's old nemesis John O'Neill, they produced a television advertisement accusing Kerry of lying about his record in Vietnam. Among the charges were claims that he had wounded himself in order to be sent home, that he had murdered a fleeing teenage civilian in one attack, and that he had fled during battle. None of the charges was substantiated; all were contradicted by the public records held in the Pentagon.

When the ads were first aired they created a sensation among right-wing talk radio and cable television personalities. Because they did not seem to be getting much attention outside of anti-Democratic circles, the Kerry campaign did not initially respond forcefully. It

John Kerry stumps with his vice-presidential running mate, Senator John Edwards of North Carolina, on the 2004 campaign trail. *(AP Photo)*

was unclear if they thought the charges were so outlandish that they would be ignored, or if the campaign was holding back its money for the fall. But it was soon obvious that not responding quickly and forcefully was a mistake. Cable and radio shows were eager to book the leaders of the anti-Kerry group, which allowed them to repeatedly play the ad at no cost to the group. This made the charges well known. By the time an editor of a Chicago newspaper who was present at the events covered in the ad gave an interview that negated all of the charges, the attacks had badly damaged Kerry's popularity. One of his strongest assets had been tarnished, and his poll numbers began to drop.

The best opportunity to control the damage was the series of three debates held in October. Back in high

Senator Kerry and President George W. Bush shake hands
before their first debate on September 30, 2004. *(AP Photo)*

school at St. Paul's and college at Yale, Kerry had developed his debating skills and trained himself to research and understand all sides of an issue as well as to present the issue carefully and logically. This training can lead Kerry to over-examine issues, to see the complexities and nuance in every issue. This habit became a problem in the campaign of 2004 when President George W. Bush and other Republicans accused Kerry of "flip-flopping." Even opponents of Bush, those critical of the results of his decision making, agreed that he did project decisiveness. Kerry's careful thinking did not pay off in front of large audiences—they wanted sound bites.

The three debates with George Bush occurred over the last weeks of the campaign. After each one, the polls showed that most Americans thought Kerry had won. However, he was not able to sustain his momentum in the face of the well-organized Bush campaign.

By the last weeks of the campaign, Bush had opened a sizable lead. But as election day neared, it appeared that the race was tightening. The biggest issue was the war in Iraq and how it should be resolved. No president who has chosen to run for reelection during a war has ever been defeated, and in the end, President Bush won another term to carry out his policies.

John Kerry continues to hold his seat in the U.S. Senate. He has a lifetime of experience to bring to bear on critical issues of the day. He has not ruled out another run for the presidency in the future. Experience has proven that it is never wise to underestimate him.

Timeline

1943	John F. Kerry is born in Denver, Colorado, on December 11.
1954	Kerry family moves to Berlin; Kerry sent to boarding school in Switzerland.
1957	Kerry enters Fessenden School.
1958	Enters St. Paul's school.
1962	Meets John F. Kennedy; enters Yale.
1966	Graduates Yale; joins the navy.
1967	Assigned to duty on the USS *Gridley* in June.
1968	Assigned to swift boat duty in Vietnam in November.
1969	Leaves Vietnam in April.
1970	Marries Julia Thorne.
1971	Testifies before the U.S. Senate; VVAW march on Washington.
1972	Defeated in run for the House of Representatives.
1982	Kerry and Julia Thorne separate; Kerry is elected lieutenant governor of Massachusetts.
1984	Elected to the U.S. Senate.
1995	Marries Teresa Heinz.
1996	Defeats William Weld in reelection campaign.
2004	Nominated for president of the United States by the Democratic Party.

Sources

CHAPTER ONE: Family and Youth

p. 10, "city upon a hill," Francis J. Bremer, *John Winthrop: America's Forgotten Founding Father* (New York: Oxford University Press, 2003), 29.

p. 13, "astonishing results," Martin Baron, preface to *John F. Kerry: The Complete Biography by the Boston Globe Reporters Who Know Him Best*, by Michael Kranish, Brian C. Mooney, and Nina J. Easton (New York: PublicAffairs, 2004), xiii.

p. 14, "He had made . . ." Michael Kranish, Brian C. Mooney, and Nina J. Easton, *John F. Kerry: The Complete Biography by the Boston Globe Reporters Who Know Him Best* (New York: PublicAffairs, 2004), 6.

p. 15, "I remember . . ." Ibid., 19.

p. 16-17, "was all part . . ." Ibid., 21.

p. 17, "My dad was sort of . . ." Michael Kranish, "A Privileged Youth, a Taste for Risk," *Boston Globe*, June 15, 2003.

p. 17, "I always . . ." Evan Thomas, "The Solitary Soldier," *Newsweek*, August 2, 2004, 34.

p. 17, "We didn't . . ." Ibid.

p. 17, "The reticence . . ." Joe Klein, "Inside the Mind of John Kerry," *Time*, August 2, 2004, 34.

p. 18, "He went into the State . . ." Douglas Brinkley, *Tour of*

Duty (New York: William Morrow, 2003), 29.

p. 19-20, "This book is the result . . ." Richard Kerry, *The Star-Spangled Mirror: America's Image of Itself and the World,* (Savage, MD: Rowman & Littlefield, 1990), ix.

p. 20, "The observation that Americans . . ." Ibid., x.

p. 21, "Those kids . . ." Thomas, "Solitary," 34.

p. 21, "He has developed . . ." Ibid., 35.

p. 21-22, "My parents were fabulous . . ." Kranish, "A Privileged Youth."

p. 22, "was a great . . ." Ibid.

p. 23, "I thought this was . . ." Kranish, *John F. Kerry,* 27.

p. 23, "He has always been . . ." James Fallows, "When George Meets John," *Atlantic Monthly,* July-August 2004, 76.

p. 24, "one of the most brilliant . . ." Kranish, "A Privileged Youth."

p. 25, "We were comfortable . . ." Brinkley, *Tour of Duty,* 33.

p. 26, "This guy is standing . . ." Kranish, "A Privileged Youth."

CHAPTER TWO: Yale

p. 27, "John loved . . ." Fallows, "When George Meets John," 76.

p. 27-28, "John would clearly . . ." Kranish, "A Privileged Youth."

p. 28, "I remember the ripple . . ." Brinkley, *Tour of Duty,* 51.

p. 29, "We were walking . . ." Ibid., 52.

p. 29, "It was a huge . . ." Ibid.

p. 29, "I was a capable . . ." Ibid., 47.

p. 29-30, "was a great . . ." Ibid.

p. 32, "I tried to offer a full . . ." Brinkley, *Tour of Duty,* 47.

p. 33, "I don't know . . ." Kranish, "A Privileged Youth."

p. 33, "destined to do . . ." Ibid.

p. 34, "We think of politicians . . ." Alexandra Robbins, "Powerful Secrets," *Vanity Fair,* July 2004, 157.

p. 35, "He just kind of . . ." Kranish, *John F. Kerry,* 60.

p. 36, "We need no ringing call . . ." Ibid., 52.

p. 36, "We have not really lost . . ." Ibid., 54.

p. 37, "the speech . . ." Joe Klein, "The Long War of John Kerry," *New Yorker,* December 2, 2002, http://www.newyorker.com/archive/content/?040126fr_archive02.

p. 37, "Our decisions were all about . . ." Ibid.

p. 37, "We have the naïve reasons . . ." Laura Blumenfeld, "The Vietnam Vet, Leaving No One Behind," *Washington Post,* July 29, 2004.

p. 37, "because he wanted . . ." Ibid.

CHAPTER THREE: Vietnam

p. 39, "I was not meant . . ." Brinkley, *Tour of Duty,* 65.

p. 41, "hair raising," Ibid., 72.

p. 41, "Hey, hey . . ." Ibid., 62.

p. 41-42, "It seemed . . ." Ibid.

p. 42-43, "I was responsible . . ." Kranish, *John F. Kerry,* 74-75.

p. 44, "Some superficial damage . . ." Erik Durschmied, *The Hinge Factor: How Chance and Stupidity Have Changed History* (New York: Arcade Publishing Company, 1999), 318.

p. 45, "empty, bitter, angry . . ." Kranish, *John F. Kerry,* 65.

p. 46, "It was awful . . ." Brinkley, *Tour of Duty,* 97.

p. 48-49, "We opened fire . . ." Ibid., 147-148.

p. 49, "Where is the enemy?" Michael Kranish, "Heroism, and Growing Concern About War," *Boston Globe,* June 16, 2003.

p. 50, "Suddenly, in a flash . . ." Brinkley, *Tour of Duty,* 216.

p. 51, "we were literally . . ." Kranish, "Heroism."

CHAPTER FOUR: Vietnam Veterans Against the War

p. 54, "I thought it was time . . ." Ibid.

p. 55, "citizen's caucus," Kranish, *John F. Kerry,* 114.

p. 56, "Miss Julia Stimson Thorne . . ." Paul Alexander, *The Candidate* (New York: Riverhead Books, 2002), 41.

p. 57, "While campaigning for Father Drinan . . ." "Angry War Veteran," *New York Times,* April 23, 1971.

p. 57-58, "was basically my concept . . ." Gerald Nicosia,

Home to War: A History of the Vietnam Veterans' Movement (New York: Crown Publishers, 2001), 98.

p. 58, "became the unofficial . . ." Michael Kranish, "With Antiwar Role, High Visibility," *Boston Globe,* June 16, 2003.

p. 58, "still a moderate . . ." "Angry War Veteran."

p. 58, "Nixon aides . . ." Kranish, "With Antiwar Role, High Visibility."

p. 59, "Destroy the young . . ." Ibid.

p. 59, "How do you ask . . ." John Kerry testifying before Senate Foreign Relations Committee, "Vietnam War Veteran John Kerry's Testimony Before the Senate Foreign Relations Committee, April 22, 1971, http://www.richmond.edu/~ebolt/history398/JohnKerryTestimony.html

p. 60, "appalled, angry . . ." Brinkley, *Tour of Duty,* 373.

p. 61, "I don't remember . . ." Kranish, "With Antiwar Role, High Visibility."

p. 61, "the type of person . . ." Kranish, *John F. Kerry,* 134.

p. 62, "Here is where we . . ." Ibid.

p. 62, "has been very . . ." Ibid., 137.

CHAPTER FIVE: The Years in Exile

p. 65, "Politics has always . . ." Brian C. Mooney, *Boston Globe,* "First Campaign Ends in Defeat," June 18, 2003.

p. 65, "an old mill city . . ." Paul Tsongas, *The Road From Here: Liberalism and Realities in the 1980s* (New York: Knopf, 1981), 5.

p. 66, "I can understand . . ." Mooney, "First Campaign."

p. 68, "put the good name . . ." Kranish, *John F. Kerry,* 155.

p. 69-70, "most people would have . . ." Mooney, "First Campaign."

p. 70, "That's a stereotype . . ." Jeffrey Toobin, "Kerry's Trials: What the candidate learned as a lawyer," *New Yorker,* May 10, 2004, http://www.newyorker.com/fact/content/?040510fa_fact1.

p. 70, "always had a prosecutor's . . ." Ibid.

p. 70-71, "To become first . . ." Ibid.

p. 72, "Kerry told me . . ." Ibid.

p. 72, "The victim was . . ." Ibid.

p. 73, "They represented . . ." Ibid.

p. 74, "February 1980 . . ." Julia Thorne with Larry Rothstein, *You Are Not Alone: Words of Experience and Hope for the Journey Through Depression* (New York: HarperPerennial, 1993), 1-2.

CHAPTER SIX: Lieutenant Governor

p. 76-77, "As he began . . ." Brian C. Mooney, "Taking One Prize, and then a Bigger One," *Boston Globe,* June 19, 2003.

p. 78, "I tried to be . . ." Kranish, *John F. Kerry,* 185.

p. 78, "When I get . . ." Klein, "The Long War of John Kerry."

p. 80, "But it was tricky . . ." Mooney, "Taking One Prize."

p. 80, "it was the right . . ." Ibid.

p. 80, "When [Kerry] is in . . ." Fallows, "When George Meets John," 76.

p. 81, "If you felt that . . ." Mooney, "Taking One Prize."

p. 81, "You impugn the . . ." Ibid.

CHAPTER SEVEN: The Senate

p. 82, "He wanted to . . ." Klein, "The Long War of John Kerry."

p. 82-83, "I think I got something . . ." Lois Romano, "John Kerry, Coming Full Circle," *Washington Post,* February 21, 1985.

p. 84, "I came to do a . . ." Dale Russakoff, "Shifting Within Party to Gain His Footing," *Washington Post,* July 26, 2004.

p. 84, "about war and peace . . ." Ibid.

p. 84, "That just isn't . . ." Ibid.

p. 84, "have been usually . . ." Toobin, "Kerry's Trials."

p. 85, "Vietnam veteran . . ." John Aloysius Farrell, "With Probes, Making his Mark," *Boston Globe,* June 20, 2003.

p. 86, "The Sandinistas' . . ." Ibid.

p. 87, "It was like a . . ." Ibid.

p. 89, "I will tell you . . ." Ibid.
p. 89, "He was told early . . ." Ibid.

CHAPTER EIGHT: Close Call

p. 94, "the most important . . ." Kranish, *John F. Kerry,* 255.
p. 94, "My greatest fear . . ." Ibid., 256.
p. 95, "we are talking . . ." Ibid., 259.
p. 96, "I asked a lot . . ." John Aloysius Farrell, "At the Center of Power, Seeking the Summit," *Boston Globe,* June 21, 2003.
p. 97, "I thought that . . ." Russakoff, "Shifting Within Party."
p. 98, "He has a capacity . . ." Ibid.
p. 98, "delighted by the . . ." Kranish, *John F. Kerry,* 290.
p. 101, "in terms of effectiveness . . ." Russakoff, "Shifting Within Party."
p. 101, "I know something . . ." Fallows, "When George Meets John," 78.
p. 101, "A lot of people thought . . ." Amanda Ripley, "The Not So Favorite Son," *Time,* August 2, 2004, 42.

CHAPTER NINE: Political Culmination

p. 103, "This is no . . ." Kranish, *John F. Kerry,* 326.
p. 104, "boldly and bravely . . ." Ibid., 327.
p. 105, "face those questions . . ." Ibid.
p. 108, "no evidence of resumed . . ." Fareed Zakaria, "We Had Good Intel—The U.N.'s," *Newsweek,* February 8, 2004, 39.
p. 109, "The capture of Saddam . . ." Kranish, *John F. Kerry,* 373.
p. 111, "I'm John Kerry . . ." John Kerry, Speech Transcript, *Washington Post,* July 20, 2004.
p. 111, "taught me . . ." Ibid.

Bibliography

Alexander, Paul. *The Candidate*. New York: Riverhead Books, 2004.

Blumenfeld, Laura. "The Vietnam Vet, Leaving No One Behind." *Washington Post*, July 29, 2004.

Bremer, Francis J. *John Winthrop: America's Forgotten Founding Father*. New York: Oxford University Press, 2003.

Brinkley, Douglas. *Tour of Duty*. New York: William Morrow, 2003.

Durschmied, Erik. *The Hinge Factor: How Chance and Stupidity Have Changed History*. New York: Arcade Publishing Company, 1999.

Fallows, James. "When George Meets John." *Atlantic Monthly*, July-August 2004, 67-80.

Farrell, John Aloysius. "At the center of power, seeking the summit." *Boston Globe*. June 21, 2003.

————. "With probes, making his mark." *Boston Globe*, June 20, 2003.

Kerry, John. Speech Transcript, *Washington Post*, July 20, 2004.

Kerry, John. Testimony before Senate Foreign Relations Committee, "Vietnam War Veteran John Kerry's Testimony Before the Senate Foreign Relations Committee," April 22, 1971. http://www.richmond.edu/~ebolt/history398/JohnKerryTestimony.html.

Kerry, John and Vietnam Veterans Against the War. *The New Soldier*. Edited by David Thorne and George Butler. New York: Macmillan, 1971.

Kerry, Richard. *The Star-Spangled Mirror: America's Image of Itself and the World*. Savage, MD: Rowman & Littlefield, 1990.

Klein, Joe. "Inside the Mind of John Kerry." *Time*, August 2, 2004.

————. "The Long War of John Kerry." *New Yorker,* December 2, 2002. http://www.newyorker.com/archive/ content/?040126fr_archive02.

Kranish, Michael. "Heroism, and growing concern about war." *Boston Globe,* June 16, 2003.

————. "With antiwar role, high visibility." *Boston Globe,* June 16, 2003.

————. "A privileged youth, a taste for risk." *Boston Globe,* June 15, 2003.

Kranish, Michael, Brian C. Mooney, and Nina Easton. *John Kerry: The Complete Biography by the Boston Globe Reporters Who Know Him Best.* New York: PublicAffairs, 2004.

Mooney, Brian C. "Taking one prize, and then a bigger one." *Boston Globe,* June 19, 2004.

————. "First Campaign ends in defeat." *Boston Globe,* June 18, 2004.

New York Times, "Angry War Veteran," April 23, 1971.

Newsweek, "The Demonstrators: Why? How Many?" November 1, 1965.

Nicosia, Gerald. *Home to War: A History of the Vietnam Veterans' Movement.* New York: Crown Publishers, 2001.

Oliphant, Thomas. "The Kerry You Should Know." *The American Prospect,* August 2004.

Ripley, Amanda. "The Not So Favorite Son." *Time,* August 2, 2004.

Robbins, Alexandra. "Powerful Secrets." *Vanity Fair,* July 2004, 115-120, 156-159.

Romano, Lois. "Sharp Focus on Lt. Kerry's Four Months Under Fire." *Washington Post,* April 23, 2004.

————. "John Kerry, Coming Full Circle." *Washington Post,* February 21, 1985.

Russakoff, Dale. "Shifting Within Party to Gain His Footing." *Washington Post,* July 26, 2004.

Thomas, Evan. "The Solitary Soldier." *Newsweek,* August 2, 2004.

————. "I'm a Good Closer." *Newsweek,* February 2, 2004, 26-28.

Thorne, Julia with Larry Rothstein. *You Are Not Alone: Words of Experience and Hope for the Journey Through Depression.* New York: HarperPerennial, 1993.

Toobin, Jeffrey. "Annals of Law: What the candidate learned as a lawyer." *New Yorker,* May 10, 2004, http://www.newyorker.com/fact/content/?040510fa_fact1.

Tsongas, Paul. *The Road from Here: Liberalism and Realities in the 1980s.* New York: Knopf, 1981.

Woodward, Bob. *Veil: The Secret Wars of the CIA, 1981–1987.* New York: Simon and Schuster, 1987.

Zakaria, Fareed. "We Had Good Intel—the U.N.'s." *Newsweek,* February 9, 2004, 39.

Web sites

http://www.johnkerry.com/
John Kerry's official campaign site, now a home for political activism.

http://kerry.senate.gov/
John Kerry's online office.

http://www.boston.com/globe/nation/packages/kerry/
The online home of the *Boston Globe* series on Kerry—with photos.

http://www.pbs.org/wgbh/amex/vietnam/
PBS's extensive site about the Vietnam War.

http://www.pbs.org/battlefieldvietnam/
Another look at the Vietnam War, also from PBS.

Index

Minh, Ho Chi, 30
Morse, F. Bradford, 64
Mueller, Robert, 23
Murphy, Evelyn, 77

Nader, Ralph, 59
New York Times, 55, 57-58
Nixon, Richard, 24, 50, 58-
   59, 62-63, 65, 67-70, 112
Noriega, Manuel, 90
North, Oliver, 87-88, *88*

O'Neill, John, 61, 112
O'Neill, Thomas P., III, 75,
   76
Ortega, Daniel, 86

Pershing, John J., 22
Pershing, Richard, 22, 34-35,
   44-45
Philbin, Philip J., 55
Pines, Lois, 77

Rasmussen, Jim, 53, 109-110
Reagan, Ronald, 81, 85-89
Rosenblith, Ronald F., 69-70

San Francisco Chronicle, 41
September 11, 2001, 103-106
Shannon, James, 80-81
Short, Frederick, 51-52
Smith, Francis, 72-73
Smith, Fred, 34-35, 37, *40*
Smith, Gaddis, 29-32, 37

Sragow, Roanne, 73
Stalin, Joseph, 18
Stanberry, William (Chip), 27-
   28, 33-34

Terrell, Jack, 87-88
Thorne, David, 35, 37, *40,*
   40-42, 46, 80
Thorne, Julia (first wife), 35,
   46, 48, 55-57, *56,* 64-65,
   73-74, 78-79, 91
Tobin, John, 71
Tonkin Gulf Resolution, 31
Tsongas, Paul, 69, *69,* 79-80

USS *Gridley,* 42-43, 45-46

Vietnam Veterans Against the
   War, 57-63
Vietnam War, 30-38, 39-53,
   54-63, 80-81, 87, 94-98,
   112-113

Walinsky, Adam, 55
Washington Post, 37
Weld, William F., 91, 100-
   101, *101,*
Westmoreland, William, 44
Winthrop, Clara, 22
Winthrop, John, 10, *11*
Winthrop, Serita, 29
World War I, 22
World War II, 10-11, 13-15,
   18-20, 29, 35